THE PRACTICAL FLOWER GARDEN

BY

HELENA RUTHERFURD ELY

AUTHOR OF "A WOMAN'S HARDY GARDEN,"
"ANOTHER HARDY GARDEN BOOK," ETC.

WITH ILLUSTRATIONS MADE FROM PHOTOGRAPHS TAKEN IN THE AUTHOR'S
GARDEN, AND IN THE "CONNECTICUT GARDEN"

1913

British Library Cataloguing-in-Publication Data
A catalogue record for this book is available from the
British Library

A Short History of Gardening

Gardening is the practice of growing and cultivating plants as part of horticulture more broadly. In most domestic gardens, there are two main sets of plants; 'ornamental plants', grown for their flowers, foliage or overall appearance – and 'useful plants' such as root vegetables, leaf vegetables, fruits and herbs, grown for consumption or other uses. For many people, gardening is an incredibly relaxing and rewarding pastime, ranging from caring for large fruit orchards to residential yards including lawns, foundation plantings or flora in simple containers. Gardening is separated from farming or forestry more broadly in that it tends to be much more labour-intensive; involving *active participation* in the growing of plants.

Home-gardening has an incredibly long history, rooted in the 'forest gardening' practices of prehistoric times. In the gradual process of families improving their immediate environment, useful tree and vine species were identified, protected and improved whilst undesirable species were eliminated. Eventually foreign species were also selected and incorporated into the 'gardens.' It was only after the emergence of the first civilisations that wealthy individuals began to create gardens for aesthetic purposes. Egyptian tomb paintings from around 1500 BC provide some of the earliest physical evidence of ornamental horticulture and landscape design; depicting lotus ponds surrounded by symmetrical rows of acacias and palms. A notable example of an ancient ornamental garden was the 'Hanging Gardens of Babylon' – one of the Seven Wonders of the Ancient World.

Ancient Rome had dozens of great gardens, and Roman estates tended to be laid out with hedges and vines and contained a wide variety of flowers – acanthus, cornflowers, crocus, cyclamen, hyacinth, iris, ivy, lavender, lilies, myrtle, narcissus, poppy, rosemary and violets as well as statues and sculptures. Flower beds were also popular in the courtyards of rich Romans. The Middle Ages represented a period of decline for gardens with aesthetic purposes however. After the fall of Rome gardening was done with the purpose of growing **medicinal herbs** and/or decorating church **altars**. It was mostly monasteries that carried on the tradition of garden design and horticultural techniques during the medieval period in Europe. By the late thirteenth century, rich Europeans began to grow gardens for leisure as well as for medicinal herbs and vegetables. They generally surrounded them with walls – hence, the 'walled garden.'

These gardens advanced by the sixteenth and seventeenth centuries into symmetrical, proportioned and balanced designs with a more classical appearance. Gardens in the renaissance were adorned with sculptures (in a nod to Roman heritage), topiary and fountains. These fountains often contained 'water jokes' – hidden cascades which suddenly soaked visitors. The most famous fountains of this kind were found in the Villa d'Este (1550-1572) at Tivoli near Rome. By the late seventeenth century, European gardeners had started planting new flowers such as tulips, marigolds and sunflowers.

These highly complex designs, largely created by the aristocracy slowly gave way to the individual gardener however – and this is where this book comes in! Cottage Gardens first emerged during the Elizabethan times, originally created by poorer workers to provide themselves with food and herbs, with flowers planted amongst them for decoration. Farm workers were generally provided with cottages set in a small garden—about an acre—where they could grow food, keep pigs, chickens and often bees; the latter necessitating the planting of decorative pollen flora. By Elizabethan times there was more prosperity, and thus more room to grow flowers. Most of the early cottage garden flowers would have had practical uses though —violets were spread on the floor (for their pleasant scent and keeping out vermin); calendulas and primroses were both attractive and used in cooking. Others, such as sweet william and hollyhocks were grown entirely for their beauty.

Here lies the roots of today's home-gardener; further influenced by the 'new style' in eighteenth century England which replaced the more formal, symmetrical 'Garden à la française'. Such gardens, close to works of art, were often inspired by paintings in the classical style of landscapes by Claude Lorraine and Nicolas Poussin. The work of Lancelot 'Capability' Brown, described as 'England's greatest gardener' was particularly influential. We hope that the reader is inspired by this book, and the long and varied history of gardening itself, to experiment with some home-gardening of their own. Enjoy.

THIS BOOK IS DEDICATED TO
MY BEST FRIEND AND
SEVEREST CRITIC

PREFACE

IN this little book are given the results of my experience in practical work in the flower garden during the last five years, in caring for the grass and evergreens, arranging flowers to secure constant color effects, raising plants and trees from seeds, and the use of fertilizers most suited to the needs of the various plants and productive of the best results.

The chapter on the Wild Garden owes its being to the maker of the "Connecticut Garden," who has given me frequent opportunities of watching its development, and much of the information contained in the chapter. To him also I am indebted for the beautiful photographs which may serve as an inspiration to those who would find delight in creating a similar garden of native plants and shrubs.

March, 1911

TABLE OF CONTENTS

LIST OF ILLUSTRATIONS

LIST OF ILLUSTRATIONS

ILLUSTRATIONS IN TEXT

xii

LIST OF ILLUSTRATIONS

COLOR ARRANGEMENTS OF FLOWERS

CHAPTER I

COLOR ARRANGEMENTS OF FLOWERS

SHOULD those winter town-dwellers who are lovers of nature, and whose thoughts during the ice-bound months continually wander to their own gardens or to trees and green places which they know and love, chance to take a short trip into the near country in mid-March, a brightness and touch of warmth in the sunshine, and certain awakenings of nature, will bring to them a thrill of delight in the knowledge that " the winter is past."

Snowbanks may be lingering in dark nooks; there may still be a fringe of ice upon the brooks that wander through the woods; but in marshy places the skunk cabbage is unfolding its broad leaves; the downy buds are expanding upon the willows; many

3

maples show a tinge of the red of coming blossoms; grass that has been properly cared for is already emerald-green; crocuses and snowdrops are bravely blooming in sheltered places, and, if one gently lifts the covering of the beds where daffodils have slept through the winter, their slender green tips will be seen pushing through the brown earth. Frogs in sunny ponds are beginning to pipe their shrill song, the robins have come back, and the town-dweller returns to the noisy city of brick and stone possessed by the longing that spring calls forth, to be at work among the growing things and to watch nature as she comes to life again.

The happy owners of gardens know that now no day should be lost. With every new sun, the buds on trees and shrubs expand and the plants awaken, one by one. The ground must be prepared, seeds sown, and, in fact, the most delightful season in the gardener's life has come, for now she is inspired by hope. The many misfortunes

4

that may overtake her garden in later months have now no place in her thoughts. Rose bugs, mildew, cut-worm, rust, and the dreadful summer drought, have for her, as yet, no existence. Every seed will germinate and become a sturdy plant which will blossom the season through. All the color arrangements planned will satisfy her anticipations; the spring, summer and early autumn are to bring her ample fruition for her present labors; for the blessed new birth of imagination and hope, which comes to the nature-lover in the youth of the year, makes all things seem possible.

Even an experienced gardener is often led away by the fascinating descriptions in the plant and seedsmen's catalogues, whose pictures both fire and bewilder the imagination. And what could be more heavenly for a woman gardener than to be able to grow all these flowers and plants, and to attain the marvelous results pictured in the catalogues; to have all the space she wanted in which to grow them, to have all the men she needed—really good and efficient men—to cultivate them, and a husband who never grumbled about the amount of manure or fertilizer she used!

We who have borne the stress of many years of gardening are now generally able, when making our spring and autumn lists, to harden our hearts to the temptations offered us in the pages of the catalogues. Of course, we often want everything we see, but are able to keep ourselves within limits. We can sympathize with and understand, however, the difficulty of the young woman who is making her first garden, and know well how she often spends time and money, only to reap disappointment. When she reads in catalogues such descriptions as "Magnificent flowers, strong and robust," "A new type of phenomenally robust growth," "Magnificent and indispensable flowering plants," we know how easily she may be misled.

It is not necessary to have in her garden every plant that any one else has had, but we should endeavor to achieve our results by growing those flowers which are best suited to the locality where we live, and which give us the most remuneration for our trouble, and then, as our experience grows, gradually increase the varieties.

Of course, one often tries a new plant, from a desire to experiment or from curiosity, just as one chooses a " salad Marguerite " or a " coupe San Jacques," or other dish with a strange name, from a restaurant menu, and returns again to the old flowers, as to the simple dishes.

There will often be a visitor come to see the garden, generally a woman, who will look about critically and then remark, " I do not see such and such a flower ;" when you must acknowledge that you not only have not grown it but have never heard of it. But do not be discouraged, as such inquiries are not meant unkindly, and even

7

the largest garden has not space for every flower that can be grown.

Enough cannot be said upon the advantages of close planting, which produces not only a more even effect of color, but also an appearance of greater luxuriance. The flowers really do better when closely set, as the ground is thus shaded by the foliage, and does not become so dry as where the planting is sparse.

We should also practice intensive gardening, which provides successive crops of flowers in the same bed or border, and better utilizes every inch of space, arranging so that one flower will promptly follow another in the same place. The asters should be fine plants ready to take the places of the Canterbury bells; gladioli should be planted to bloom where the foxgloves stood; cosmos should be raised to spread its feathery branches where the tall hollyhocks have been cut down; tuberous-rooted begonias should be planted to fill later the places in the border where tulips welcomed the spring; and seedlings of annuals should be set everywhere,—not one or two of a kind planted indiscriminately, but so that each border will have masses in colors that blend.

All of this work requires much thought and experiment, opens a wide and fascinating field to the amateur, and gives an added zest to the joys of gardening.

Even before the frost has entirely left the ground, shrubs, hedges, vines, and climbing roses should be fertilized, so that the spring rains may carry the tonic directly to the roots of the plants. Manure (it no longer can be called " barnyard," since in no self-respecting barn-yard can manure be gathered today), mixed with bone meal in the proportion of five shovels to the wheelbarrow of manure, is best for the purpose.

As soon as the ground can be dug, shrubs and hardy vines should be transplanted, or set out. All soft-wooded trees, such as poplars, willows, catalpas, tulips, magnolias, as

9

well as both purple and copper beech and the larch, must also be set out in the early spring before growth begins.

Attractive plantings, made in the autumn, of shrubs and bulbs which bloom at the same time in the spring, are:

Early daffodils, which have been covered during the winter to bring them forward sooner, may be grown under and around the forsythia bushes.

The pink-flowered crab apples, of which Bechtel's, Parkman's, and Siberian are good varieties, may be planted with the long-stemmed May-flowering rose-pink tulips, mingled with crimson and white bybloem tulips and a few clumps of the pale lavender German iris springing from the grass around them, will make a lovely corner about May 15th.

Gesneriana tulips bloom at the same time as the *Spiræa Van Houttei*, and are effective together.

Columbines, with lavender and white rockets grown in quantities, together with late-

blooming white lilacs, such as Mme. Casimir-
Perier, and Marie Legraye, have been very
nice in my garden.

Azalea mollis, with late yellow tulips,
together with *Deutzia rosea* and the deliciously scented daphne, make satisfactory combinations.

Late yellow or pink tulips may be planted
around a clump of pink double-flowering
almond; and, as the German iris blooms at
the same time with the syringa, of which
Grandiflorus is the best variety, a quantity
of this iris, in many varieties, is lovely when
grown in a bed surrounding the syringa.

A beautiful shrubbery can be composed
by using weigelia, varieties Rosea and Eva
Rathke, the golden-leaved syringa, both pink
and white deutzia, Japanese snowballs, both
the golden and the variegated elder, some
Japanese maples both red and yellow-leaved,
two or three purple-leaved plums, a few cedars,
and a few retinisporas, with an occasional
Lombardy poplar at the back.

11

Such a shrubbery, now about seven years old, probably two hundred feet in length, grows along the front of a beautiful place on Long Island, and forms a lovely screen between the house and the highway, which is thus entirely shut out. The syringas, weigelias and Japanese snowballs are in full bloom at the same time, and their blossoms, together with the golden and silvery foliage of the alders and elders, the purple of the plums, and the dark green evergreens adding strength to the whole, make it a most remarkable shrubbery. It is interesting to know that this was planned unaided by a woman, although she has an excellent gardener.

During the last week of May and the first ten days of June, the gardener finds his busiest time. All the annuals must now be lifted from the seed-bed and transplanted to the places where they are to grow. The young plants must also be taken out of the hotbeds at this time, which is a work that can be

done only late in the afternoon, between four
and six o'clock, as the seedlings should have
the cool night in which to recover from the
operation of transplanting. The gladioli and
tuberoses must be set out; the weeds which
grow over night must have attention; the
grass must be cut every three or four days;
fresh crops of vegetables must be put in the
vegetable garden; and then, on some fine day,
when everything seems to need attention,
the gardener insists that the potatoes must
be cultivated, and there come moments when
one wishes that there was no such thing as
a vegetable or potato crop on the place.

The most interesting of all gardening is in
the cultivation of herbaceous plants. These
hardy perennials bloom luxuriantly, give a
wide range of color, and are of varied heights.
A great landscape architect recently told me
that in his opinion it required more intelli-
gence and ability, even with the assistance of
annuals, to keep an herbaceous border effective in color, and in good condition, than to

run an orchid house; he added the remark that, after trying new plants every year, he had found that the list of really desirable perennials and annuals did not greatly increase.

In making an herbaceous border where many different-colored plants are to be grown, the effect will be more beautiful if white flowers in quantity are planted between each of the different colors, care being taken to allow a few plants of the palest shade of each color to drift among the white, so that the transition may be less abrupt. If a plan of the planting be made in advance, the work will be easier and more successful. Heterogeneous planting is often painful. Pink and blue flowers, red, purple, and yellow, must be arranged to produce artistic effect.

Larkspurs, for instance, are far more beautiful when grown in great masses of each different shade, or with white Japanese iris and *Lilium candidum,* than in smaller clumps in a border where many other colored flowers are planted. Pale blue larkspur with the dark variety, Formosum, behind it, and pale yellow coreopsis and pale yellow calendula in the foreground, make an attractive planting.

Early one July, my baby grandson was christened in our quaint little church in the country. Larkspur, and candidum lilies, with which I have at last been able to succeed,— both of which flowers are so exquisite in the garden, and so perishable when gathered that one should always cut them judiciously,— were in their prime in wonderful quantity. And, on this great day, we were able to fill a large clothes-basket with the stalks of the lilies and the branches of the pale blue *Delphinium cœlestinum,* and take them to make the little church beautiful, without missing any from the garden.

Since there have been herbaceous borders of only one or two colors in my garden, the effect has been more beautiful and the arrangement simplified; and this plan is likely to be adhered to for some time to come. But one must always keep an eagle eye upon

15

the borders, to be sure that plants are not allowed to go to seed; for the best of gardeners often fail to realize that all flowers will bloom much longer if seed-pods are kept from forming. One of the men does every morning what I call " giving a fatherly touch to the garden." He begins at one end of the place when he first comes on duty, and with shears and basket goes through the entire garden, taking off every withered flower or leaf, thus preserving not only the neatness of the place but the perfection of the plants. This, being done regularly, is done easily, and takes hardly an hour a day.

The white border is my greatest delight; the flowers grown in it are exquisite at night as well as in the daytime.

At the back of the border are *Bocconia cordata*, the spireas, Aruncus and Gigantea, and white hollyhocks. These tall plants are followed in September by the mammoth cosmos, which is started under glass to insure

16

A group of Yuccas

its blooming before frost. Then there are *Lilium auratum, L. album,* and *L. candidum,* which bloom from June until frost, and, if planted from fifteen to eighteen inches deep, seem to succeed far better than with shallower planting. Tall spikes of *Hyacinthus candicans, Physostegia Virginica alba,* flowering in July for a month, Achillea, which generously blooms the whole summer through, white phlox, both early and late, white lupins and dictamnus, both of which bloom for a month from the middle of May, foxgloves, *Lysimachia clethroides, Campanula medium,* some clumps of white Japanese iris, and the old-time valerian, filling the air with its delicious perfume in May.

For annuals, there are stocks, sweet sultan, the white cornflower, *Cyanus albus,* Empress candytuft, snapdragons, asters and gladioli.

The pink border, or indeed an entire garden of pink flowers, is not difficult of attainment. Pink hollyhocks and cosmos, many shades

17

of phlox, *Lilium rubrum*, *L. rubellum*, and *L. magnificum*, pink lupins which are more beautiful than either the white or blue varieties and easy to raise from seed, *Incarvillea Delavayi*, *Sedum spectabile*, Canterbury bells, and some pink columbines, *Spiræa elegans* and pink dictamnus, should be planted for May blooming.

Then the pink annual larkspurs, camellia-flowered balsams, which in rich soil are wonderful plants, *Phlox Drummondi*, which flowers all summer if not allowed to seed, tuberous-rooted begonias, each plant of which is a mass of blossoms for three months, verbenas—glorified editions of the old-time verbena—which should be started under glass with the cosmos, and, if there is place for them, gladioli, so necessary for bloom in September.

The blue border is more unusual, and, although I have visited many gardens in many countries, I have never seen a plantation of blue flowers only.

Larkspurs, monkshood in early and late varieties, including the light blue variety, *Aconitum Wilsoni*, *Veronica grandiflora*, platycodon, the campanulas, varieties Persicifolia, Glomerata and Pyramidalis, and the lupins, are six perennials which would alone keep a blue border pronounced in color for three months; but when you add columbines, eupatorium, *Anchusa Italica*, *Baptisia Australis*, *Scabiosa Caucasica*, blue salvia, *Salvia azurea* and *Centaurea Cyanus*, the wonderful new blue gladioli, large-flowering ageratum and lobelia, which are always in bloom, and the faithful asters which, however, have a violet tinge, the blue border becomes a source of great interest.

A few white flowers, such as white platycodon, the feathery *Bocconia cordata*, *Lilium album*, *L. candidum*, and achillea, rather add to the beauty of the blue border and seem to make its color more lovely.

In the red border are red hollyhocks, scarlet lychnis, *Phlox Coquelicot*, *Tritoma*

19

Pfitzerii, the old-time monarda or bee balm, *Pentstemon barbatus Torreyii* about which many continually ask, " What is that beautiful flower?" scarlet *Phlox Drummondi,* the scarlet *Gladiolus Brenchleyensis,* salvia Bonfire, and cannas, and geraniums which may be added to carry out the color scheme.

There are, of course, many other beautiful flowers in these four colors; but, after several years of experiment, these lists have been found to comprise the most satisfactory plants in simplicity of culture and the amount of flowers they yield for use in the one-color border. As such borders are for effect, flowers can be gathered from them but sparingly; elsewhere in the garden should be grown both perennials and annuals in rows like vegetables, to supply flowers for cutting.

Stocks, both white and pink, gladioli in the same two colors, snapdragons, *Lilium rubellum* and *L. speciosum magnificum* can be successfully planted together, and if the stocks and snapdragons are started under glass, they can, by proper feeding, be made to bloom continually from early in June until ice forms. The lilies continue to unfold their buds for over a month, and the gladioli, if two plantings of them are made, will blossom for a long time; last summer, when grown with other flowers in my garden, the stalks of gladioli were over five feet in height, evidencing the effect of rich soil. This height also gave much beauty to the plantation.

White Japanese anemones, white tuberous-rooted begonias and tuberoses, are satisfactory when grown together; and if white May-flowering tulips be added, and the begonias started under glass in March, they will begin to bloom in June, so that this white corner will be a constant delight.

Poppies and sweet peas are the first flower seeds to be sown in the spring. It is difficult to sow the poppy thinly enough, as every seed seems to germinate, and the plants should be three inches apart, not only in order to develop and produce more flowers, but that they may continue in bloom for a longer period. Sown in large masses in all the many varieties, poppies make a wonderful show for three weeks. When the last petals have fallen, if the soil be enriched and cultivated, the poppy bed can again be made beautiful by transplanting into it young aster plants either of all shades of pink with white in the many varieties, or of purple and lavender shading through the delicate tones to white. The poppy bed in my garden is fifty feet long and eighteen feet wide, giving opportunity for a fine mass of color.

Asters, in the catalogues of annuals, are what phlox and larkspur are in the perennial family. Early in September, when the asters were really wonderful in my garden, and there seemed to be no end to them, I asked one of the gardeners how many had been transplanted. His reply was, " about ten thousand." As I rather doubted this state-

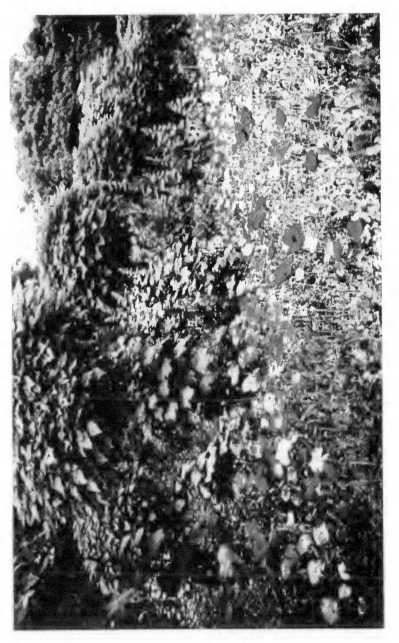

THE POPPY BED

ment, he showed me a bed of young Canterbury bells transplanted for blooming next summer, saying that he had counted them that morning, that there were nine hundred plants in the bed, and that it could be seen at a glance that there were ten times as many asters then blooming in the gardens.

For those who care for yellow and orange flowers, a border of splendid color may be made by planting the hardy perennial sunflowers, both single and double, helenium or sneeze weed, gaillardia, coreopsis and calliopsis, the marigolds and calendulas both orange and yellow, the different varieties of yellow day lilies, the tritomas, the trollius or globe flower, the California poppies, and the faithful nasturtiums. A beautiful combination with the yellow and orange is made by adding purple and magenta flowers, such as the tall liatrus or Kansas gay feather, magenta dahlias, the *Verbena venosa*, the giant ruffled magenta petunias and dark magenta phlox.

This magenta phlox, by the way, is quite a different color from that which we find in our gardens grown from self-sown seed, which is of a light purplish color. The new magenta phloxes have large heads of bloom, as well as large individual blossoms, and grow quite four feet in height.

A very effective color-planting can be made by growing dark crimson snapdragons with a tall variety of ageratum and edging the plantation with dwarf ageratum, the combination of blue and rich crimson being unusual.

There is one flower, the petunia, of which I must speak with apology because of the things I have written and said about it. The very name petunia calls to mind the ugly white and purple varieties that flourished in our mothers' gardens; but, through the skill of the hybridizer, the petunias today are among the most beautiful of all annuals, particularly the great giant ruffled and frilled varieties. The Snowstorm, a flower with a golden heart, is a continual mass of blossoms, as is also the Rosy Morn, which is pale pink as its name would indicate. There is an infinite number of other varieties, and they help us out immensely with our color effects.

Last summer, a bed of heliotrope surrounded with giant ruffled petunias in shades of lilac with golden centers was continually beautiful for nearly five months; and a carpet of Rosy Morn petunias, growing in a bed where *Lilium auratum* and *L. magnificum* raised their great stalks of lilies, entirely concealing the earth, added greatly to the effect.

The hybridizer has worked wonders, also, with the verbenas. The new varieties form trusses nearly as large as the top of a tea-cup, and give a continuous mass of color in white or pale rose until quite late in the fall, as they stand considerable frost.

The *Celosia plumosa*, or cockscomb, has become, through the skill of the growers, a wonderful flower in many colors besides the old crimson variety. It grows about three

25

feet in height, with plumes a foot in length. A brilliant yellow and a flame color are perhaps the finest. The seeds should be started in the hotbeds, to prolong the period of bloom, and the seedlings transplanted several times before being set, either in the ground, where the plants should be a foot apart, or in six-inch pots. When a foot high, they will be glad of a little bone meal, and during all their blooming period should be fed with doses of liquid manure, at least every two weeks.

The annual larkspurs, too, are greatly improved in variety, and are useful for cutting; if the seed-pods are not allowed to form, they bloom continuously all summer.

A bed of pale pink and delicate lavender annual larkspur is a lovely color combination.

Godetia, a low-growing plant about a foot in height, will thrive in poor soil, in a sunny location, and is covered with flowers—pink, white, crimson, and of every color, splashed with white.

Salpiglossis, in its many colors, also blooms continually. It does rather better if started in a hotbed, and the plants should be set about eight inches apart.

Schizanthus, which also has flowers of pink, white, rose and crimson, is continually in blossom. It is a delicate, dainty plant, and perhaps best suited for pot-culture. By sowing the seeds in March, frequently transplanting until they are finally set in an eight-inch pot, these plants will reward one for the trouble given them, and, as they are yet but little grown, excite much interest.

As we live with our gardens, plantings which once were entirely satisfactory cease in time to be all that we could wish; and we experiment and devise other arrangements, and generally find the changes make for improvement. Such a radical change was made in my little rose garden, where formerly the beds were carpeted with pansies, and a border which surrounded it was edged with pink and white sweet william. Back of this border, and surrounding the whole garden, is a hedge of pink and white altheas, which has now grown so high that the garden is quite hidden from view. The rich soil used for the roses, with the frequent watering, stimulated both pansies and sweet william to great effort. Their blossoms added to the color of the garden, and I was secretly much pleased with the effect.

One day in mid-June, when the little rose garden was in perfection of bloom, my daughter critically remarked at luncheon, "I do not like those pansies and other things in the rose-garden; everything there should grow up straight and neatly, and it is not bad if the earth is seen between the plants." Criticisms made by one's children are trying, but sometimes appropriate. Most of that afternoon I spent in the rose garden, visited it again in the evening, and slept little during that night thinking the matter over. It seemed cruel to drag out all those beautiful blooming plants. But by morning

I had decided to make the change; so, coming down very early, I found the gardener, went with him to the garden, and gave directions that every pansy and sweet william be pulled up, the beds and borders edged, and that all must be done neatly and immaculately before the men went to dinner.

Then I fled, to return only after my orders had been carried out. At first the little garden seemed bare and shorn of much beauty. But the daughter's criticism proved to be right, and now only gladioli grow among the roses, while all along the edge of the border is a row of tall tuberoses, which grow three feet in height with heads of bloom a foot in length, and perfume the night air deliciously. Every one approves the change.

We often reproach ourselves for fickleness when we find that we regard with aversion people whom we have long known and liked, because, in the lapse of years, they seem to have acquired unpleasant peculiarities, forgetting that we may ourselves have changed. May we not reproach ourselves equally when ceasing to care for plants which once we prized? Three flowers dear to me ten years ago I now entirely dislike; the crimson rambler rose, rudbeckia and *Hydrangea grandiflora.* The rudbeckia has been cast out of the garden. Nearly all of the crimson rambler roses have been taken up, leaving only a few arches and a short trellis of them, and the Pink Dorothy Perkins has been substituted; but a long hedge of hydrangeas still remain, although I now exclude them from my vision, and regard them as if they did not exist.

These brave plants are so hardy and free-blooming that they have found a place from one end of the country to the other, and are grown everywhere, yet, because of their very merits which made them so universally grown, they have become distasteful to many.

A beautiful plantation for August and September is of pink and white summer-flowering cosmos, pink and white Japanese anemones, and pink and white asters; such a border, in the garden of a relative, was, for quite six weeks, beautiful beyond my power to describe. The same flowers could be used, either all white or all pink, and would be an equally good arrangement.

This same relative makes a specialty of her spring garden. Living all the year in the country, she has the great joy of watching the wonderful phases of nature,—clouds, sunlight and shadow,—and knows the magic of the changing seasons. For six weeks in the spring her garden seems as if touched by a fairy wand, so exquisite are its colors.

It is not large, and much of the work is done by her own hands. She is indefatigable in having her borders made over at the proper intervals and in keeping the soil in good condition. When, in the autumn, a border is re-made and the perennials planted, the bulbs are then set and remain until the border is again taken up. The bulbs are planted from four to six inches deep, and, at the end of May or first of June, annuals are planted over and about them. The planting is so close that it remains a mystery to me how a trowel can ever be put into the soil without cutting a bulb.

In the border where, later, larkspur, valerian, *Anchusa Italica* and blue annuals bloom, there are, in early spring, the large white crocus and the lovely blue scilla.

In a yellow border, the daffodils, Emperor and Empress, are followed by early single yellow tulips and late double yellow tulips.

The borders on either side of a path are filled with early white tulips, to be followed by the Cottage Maid, which is pale pink. As the petals of the pale pink tulip fall, the late-blooming Isabella, a large, double pink tulip almost as large as a peony, comes into flower, and is in turn followed by the exquisite Picotee, which remains in bloom for nearly three weeks, and is, at first, white faintly tinged with pink, becoming at last almost a

32

A hedge of Hydrangeas

light American Beauty rose color. Along the edge of this border *Narcissus albus plenus odoratus* and *N. poeticus odoratus* are grown in two rows.

Another border is filled with the scarlet and white Pottebakker tulips, and edged with *Narcissus poeticus*.

Still another border contains Sulphur Phœnix daffodils in pale yellow and white, with the bright yellow Emperor, hyacinths in pale blue, blush-pink and white, and is also edged with *Narcissus poeticus*.

A very lovely pink and yellow border is filled with early and late varieties of daffodils and early and late pink tulips.

All these bulbs are planted by the thousands, and the quantity of flowers and length of bloom with the arrangement of colors, make this spring garden far more beautiful than the best I have ever seen elsewhere.

Some suggestions for color-planting are:
Ageratum, variety, Princess Pauline, in a

bed edged with sweet alyssum, variety, Carpet of Snow, both of which must be slightly trimmed from time to time, to be kept blooming.

Scarlet verbena, Defiance, in beds edged with the same sweet alyssum.

Lobelia fulgens, variety, Queen Victoria, having scarlet flowers with bronze foliage, the bed being edged with *Centaurea gymnocarpa*, which is a silvery white plant.

Browallia, speciosa major which is deep blue in color, grown with dwarf yellow snapdragons.

Tagetes, a very dwarf yellow and brown marigold, grown with heliotrope of some large-flowering dwarf variety of dark color.

Snowstorm petunia and ageratum, variety, Princess Pauline.

Petunias in all shades of magenta and magenta splashed with white, with calendulas growing back of them, and behind the calendulas African marigolds.

A quantity of the nicotianas planted to-

An old-time entrance

gether with *N. affinis*, white; *N. Sanderæ* hybrids of many colors with *N. sylvestris*, white; red tuberous-rooted begonias with lobelia, Crystal Palace, deep blue.

Canna, President Meyer, of a bright red, with bronze foliage, growing four feet high, planted with *Impatiens Sultani*, surrounding them.

Dracæna indivisa, with Rosy Morn petunia.

Pennisetum, the purple fountain grass, planted with the orchid-flowered Canna, Wyoming, which bears immense spikes of orange flowers and has bronze foliage.

The literature in all languages upon gardening, and the references to gardens in poetry and prose, both ancient and modern, as cultivated, restful, romantic and beautiful places, is infinite. In the Old Testament many allusions are to be found. We read of " the garden of nuts," " the garden of herbs," and " the garden of cucumbers."

It is a fancy of many women today to have an herb garden, but the cucumber, in the time of the prophet Isaiah, who speaks of a lodge in a garden of cucumbers, and of Baruch, who says " like a scarecrow in a garden of cucumber, which keepeth nothing away," must have been a different vegetable from the one we now cultivate under that name.

We read that " the garden causeth the things that are sown in it to spring forth," and the similes, " as gardens by the riverside," and " like a watered garden," are refreshing mental pictures to those who know the heat and dryness of the East.

Every garden has its particular charm, and rarely is one to be seen from which we can turn without having gained some new idea of color arrangement, of certain plants in wonderful perfection, or of something which gives delight and inspiration. The little gardens about laborers' cottages, where the few flowers mean so much to the man or woman who cares for them in moments before or after a long day's toil, touch the heart as

36

no great gardens can, although the latter may be more complete with all that nature and art combined are able to accomplish.

Every lover of flowers has her own ideas upon the subject of gardening. My ideal garden is one a little distance from the house, and so surrounded by trees and enclosed by hedges that the windows of the house cannot look down upon it;—a lovely out-of-doors room, as it were, neat and orderly like the rooms of the house, where every plant is brought to its highest development and nature trained by man gives constant and luxuriant bloom, where the green setting of trees, hedges, box-edging and fine turf, and the colors blending without a jarring note, fill one with a sense of delight and thanksgiving for the beauty of the spot; a place where one may walk or talk, read or work, quite unobserved, with the sunshine all around, yet seated in cool shade, and with the murmuring of falling water and the exquisite notes of the song sparrow, or the liquid call of the catbird in one's ears. Where on this earth can any place be found more exquisite and peaceful? Into such a garden Maud may have been called by her lover, and to such a little Paradise Solomon may have referred in his Songs of Songs where he sings of a " garden enclosed."

SOME GREEN THINGS OF
THE EARTH

CHAPTER II

THE chief beauty of any country place, whether it be but an acre in extent or a great estate, will always consist in its trees and evergreens, its shrubs, hedges and lawns. A country place may be entirely beautiful where no flowers are grown, if the trees and shrubbery are well planted and the lawns are in fine condition; but house and garden, however well arranged, will fail greatly in attraction if the setting which surrounds them is unworthy.

The making of lawns is a subject demanding a book by itself, and excellent books have been written giving all possible information for those who wish to make their lawns or grass paths. It is therefore my purpose to give only my own experiences in keeping the grass in good condition.

THE PRACTICAL FLOWER GARDEN

When a person has once become interested in preserving the turf about her place, it will be found a most engrossing, and delightful occupation. Until this interest is aroused, many who are really excellent flower or vegetable gardeners may be both ignorant of the care of the grass and unobservant of its condition. A man who was an excellent flower gardener once said to me, "I do not bother with the grass except to keep it cut; so long as there is 'something green,' I am satisfied." Probably the " something green " was in his case, as in many others, composed of chicory, moss, plantain, dandelion and sparse grass. Where the turf is thick and fine, there is not much place for weeds to root, and on a fine surface of grass a weed is immediately apparent to the watchful eye.

Many professional gardeners, as well as those who are amateurs, seem to think that if in winter they scatter over the lawn manure, which is often crude and raw from not being sufficiently decomposed, therefore having in it many seeds of weeds,—if they rake this off in the spring and then put the lawn-mower to work, regardless of dry weather, or whether the lawn may be so burned by drought that there is really no grass to mow, they have done all that is needed. We have, all of us, I fancy, seen men mowing sun-burned lawns, and wondered why they were doing so—and also watering the grass at a time and in ways which were more harmful than not. It requires a great deal of water to wet sod even one inch in depth; and, when only the top of the earth is wet, the roots of the grass, instead of sinking deeper, as they should, come to the surface to find the moisture, with the result that any grass so treated will eventually become burned.

The lawn that has been properly put down in the first instance is not difficult to keep in excellent condition, and with even slight care its yearly improvement should be great and continuous. Early in the spring the ground should be gone over carefully and every weed taken out by the roots. These will be found to be mostly dandelions and plantain. When the weeds have been taken out, the workman, who should have a box of grass seed by his side, should put a pinch of seed into the hole where the weed has been and press the sod well down. When the whole lawn has been thus gone over, it is well then to sow seed thinly broadcast and roll it in thoroughly. Two men can push a three-hundred-and-fifty-pound roller, which is heavy enough to keep the grass in good condition. Sufficient emphasis cannot be laid upon the advisability of frequent rolling for the grass. The roots, which have been disturbed by thawing and freezing or long drought, are thus firmly set in the earth, and the whole surface of the lawn made compact and even.

When the newly sown grass seed has germinated and the young grass is a couple of inches high, cottonseed meal can be sown broadcast with great advantage. This may

ONE OF THE LONG GRASS PATHS

be sown so that the grass has a yellow look; in case no rain follows within a day, the hose should be attached to the sprinklers and the water turned on so that the cottonseed meal is at once watered into the roots of the new grass. I was first told of the benefit of cottonseed meal to grass about ten years ago by a gentleman who sat next to me at dinner. He told me, to my great surprise, that it would make two blades of grass grow where only one had been before, and during all these ten years I have used it on my own lawns and paths to the greatest advantage. In fact, some seasons my men have asked me not to use it, for it causes such a growth that if there is sufficient rain during the spring the grass must be mown every three days.

About May 1st, a further tonic may be given to the lawn by sowing broadcast finely ground bone meal and wood ashes mixed together, equal parts of each to the bushel, and sown so as to give the lawn a light gray color. This should be again watered in and rolled. About a ton of cottonseed meal to the acre, and the same quantity of the bone meal and wood ashes mixture, may be used to advantage.

This treatment should carry the lawns and grass paths through even our hot and dry summers; and if there are places worn by much use, a solution of nitrate of soda—one pound of nitrate to forty gallons of water— can be applied, which will have an immediate effect. This must also be thoroughly watered in should there not be rain within twenty-four hours after its application.

Another excellent tonic for the grass is hen manure mixed with earth, equal parts of each, and scattered over the grass at the rate of a bushel of the mixture for about a thousand square feet of surface. This also will produce great growth.

Sometimes, in August, if the lawn looks a little worn and badly, it may be given another dose of the cottonseed meal, which must again be watered in thoroughly.

The guardian of the garden

Along towards the end of June and in July, crab grass and orchard grass appear, both of which are coarse in quality and rusty in color; these grasses seed themselves and spread rapidly over large areas. They must be dug or pulled up ruthlessly, roots and all at once, for if allowed to remain, they would entirely ruin a lawn in three years' time. The bare places can be re-sodded or sown with grass seed, the smaller areas being preferably sodded. It is only by keeping careful watch, and exterminating these horrid grasses upon their first appearance, that they may be kept out of our lawns.

In October, the grass should be gone over again most carefully and all the weeds removed. There will probably be many young dandelions, the seeds of which were blown in from neighboring fields. These must be rooted out. If moss and sorrel appear, it is a sure sign that the ground is sour and needs lime, which should then be spread over the ground broadcast during the winter, one bushel to a thousand feet of surface.

The finest grass of all for lawns is the Kentucky blue. It thrives anywhere north of Georgia upon any soil not acid, and if there is acidity it can be corrected either by the winter-sown lime or by incorporating the proper amount of lime with the soil when making the lawn. One understands how this grass derives its name, for its color in early morning and at sunset, when the light is level, is nearly as blue as the foliage of the *Retinispora squarrosa*. This grass gradually takes the place of the other grasses sown with it, and the whole area becomes of one color and texture.

For years I have used, with great success, a mixture composed of one-third each to the bushel, of Kentucky blue grass, red top and Rhode Island bent, and have recommended it to many of my friends, who have found it most satisfactory. It is particularly thriving in a limestone region. Where the soil is sandy, a mixture of Kentucky blue grass, twenty-five per cent; creeping bent, thirty per cent; Rhode Island bent, thirty per cent, and fine-leaved fescue, fifteen per cent, is recommended by Leonard Barron, an expert on the care and making of lawns. The creeping bent and fine-leaved fescue produce quickly-growing, binding grasses that withstand drought. Mr. Barron recommends the same mixture for sea-side lawns, substituting beach grass for the fine-leaved fescue. Mr. Samuel Parsons, the well-known landscape architect, told me that there were certain shady places in Trinity Churchyard, New York, rarely reached by the sun, where it had been almost impossible to get grass to grow, but that he had succeeded in getting a fine turf with wood meadow grass—(*Poa nemoralis*),—having first spread over the surface a couple of inches of fine humus or leaf-mold. This wood meadow grass will thrive in shady places where almost no other grass can be made to grow.

An attractive treatment for very shady walks is made by laying flat, irregular stones as stepping-stones, the sides of the rows of stones to be quite uneven, and the spaces filled with moss, rock fern and other rock plants.

For the last three years there has been drought in our part of the country, and hundreds of people have tramped over my grass paths, which are never watered; but the grass has resisted the drought wonderfully, and the turf remains thick and green. During dry weather the grass is allowed to grow rather long, being mown only every two weeks or so, and in August it is helped along with more cottonseed meal or the wood ashes and bone meal mixture.

It is a mistake to mow the lawn too early in the spring, as the grass does better during the summer if allowed to become five or six inches high before the first mowing, and after October it should not be cut at all.

Lawns in England are preserved for gener-

The circle at the top of the cedar walk

ations by rolling and cutting and keeping them free from weeds, with constant additions of seed and fertilizer. In this country, through carelessness and ignorance, and especially through improper preparation of the soil in making lawns, it is necessary to "take them up," as the gardener expresses it, and make them over frequently. The end of August, or September 1st, and very early in spring, are the best seasons for making a lawn. If a new lawn or grass-path is made in late August, or early in September,—the only time in the autumn when it is safe to sow grass seed,—it should be given a slight protection of straw, corn-stalks, or old manure, before the ground freezes. Then, in the spring, when this is raked off, some seed should be thinly sown and the whole very thoroughly rolled.

My own experience in making lawns has taught me that the grass sown in late summer gives a far better result the following year than the spring-made lawn. On August

26th, last year, seed was sown on a grass-path that had never been made but had just grown. The ground was uneven and the path needed grading. The sod was so good, however, that it was a wrench to take it up, and I fled from the place during the operation. Upon my return, a week after the grass seed had been sown, I found a broad, level path, already colored with a faint tinge of green. Although the drought was extreme, enough water was forthcoming to wet the ground every other day at sunset. Two or three blessed showers, each of an hour's duration, saved the grass at critical periods, and, on September 19th, less than four weeks after sowing, the grass had become so long that it was necessary to mow it, the knives of the machine being set very high.

The first week in September, two years ago, seed was sown on a grass-walk twenty feet wide, which winds for four hundred feet up a hill on a gentle curve, and ends at the top in a circle fifty feet across. The grass was watered daily, and by the end of October there was a fair turf on the walk, notwithstanding the dry autumn. The walk and the circle are bordered by cedar trees, from eight to ten feet high, which have been set touching each other. Just inside the line of cedar trees, a border about four feet wide has been made, which is planted with hardy things that thrive without other attention than keeping the weeds from choking them. In "proud pied April," daffodils, jonquils and narcissi wind like a golden ribbon through the grass at the feet of the dark cedars. Many-hued columbines follow the daffodils, and, toward the end of May, single Japanese peonies unfold their lovely petals; the peonies, being both early and late varieties, yield their blossoms for three weeks. Later, there rise the tall bocconia (*Nicotiana sylvestris*), or common tobacco, with its fragrant white flowers, and the tasselled " Lady's Riding Whip." Here also the *Gaillardia grandiflora* has found a home. But the cedar walk is seen in its glory in September and October, when the great starwort family is in its prime; and there are clumps of these flowers in each shade from dark purple to pale lilac, and white to crimson, with sumach and feathery white boltonia in among them, lining all the sides of the walk. Last autumn, in late September, a visitor standing at the lower end of this cedar walk and looking up at the green pathway enclosed by the cedars, with the hardy asters in their many shades, and the brilliant sumach, all together giving a wonderful color effect, exclaimed, " What a beautiful autumn garden!"

In the circle at the top of the hill, I hope some day to build a small, white, circular summer-house, in the form of a tiny temple, where, in late afternoon, one may sit and look over a long valley where the hills rise in every direction, and watch the sunset lights and the falling twilight; or, in the summer evenings, may climb the hill when the full moon clothes the earth with matchless beauty, and the scent of flowers from the garden below rises to perfume the air, and only the myriad insect voices of the night break the solemn stillness.

For years to come, however, there will be work without end to be done on the cedar walk: the grass must be kept free from weeds, if a tree dies it must be replaced, and there will always be space for more daffodils and hardy plants. The cedar walk is also an exquisite spot on a winter's day, when the color of the trees against the sky and the snow is more intense than at any other time, and the quiet and shelter afforded by their protecting walls of green make of this long walk a grateful refuge.

The sod nursery is a necessary requisite on a country place of any size. Sodding of large areas is to be avoided, because of the expense in buying the sod and laying it, and also because the turf is seldom so satisfactory on a large surface, when sodded, as if grown from seed. Yet the need of sod is a matter of frequent occurrence, either to border paths, or to set into the lawn in spots where wild grasses have been taken out, or to cover the place where a discarded flower-bed has been, or where the turf has become worn out through use.

For years we have taken the sod needed for these purposes from a field called the "night pasture lot," where the herd is turned at night. The field contains about fifteen acres; a slender, cold brook bordered with water-cress, the outlet of a spring, winds through it, and white-trunked sycamores and ancient elms give it great beauty. The field has probably never been ploughed, and the natural grass is fine and thick. The most distant corner of the lot is chosen, and the sod is lifted with a prayer to the gods of the garden that the farmer-husband may not discover the deed; but, alas! his eagle eye always lights upon the bare spots before new grass is grown.

Even this fine, close native grass is different in color and texture from the Kentucky blue grass used in the garden, and the sodded places can be discerned by a close observer. At last, therefore, though late in time, a sod nursery has been started, quite small to begin with, about fifty feet square. The earth was prepared in the same manner as if a lawn were to be made, was rolled and watered, and is kept mown and given the same care as the lawns and paths. As sod is removed from time to time, fertilizer is raked in and more seed sown, and thus the sod nursery will be continually renewed. As it takes about two years before the sod is sufficiently firm for use, whoever is making a new place should lose no time in preparing the sod-nursery, that sod may be ready when needed.

When cedar trees are transplanted, if heavy, flat stones are placed on the ground close around the trunks of the trees and over the roots, they will not only aid in holding the tree firmly in the ground but also help greatly in retaining the precious moisture. On my place, the cedar trees, after being transplanted, were formerly tied to stout stakes, and kept so tied for at least a year, until a friend, whose transplanted cedars always live, told me of this use of flat stones, which we have since found most effective.

One day, when looking at the wonderful cedars this friend had successfully transplanted, I ventured to remark, " You certainly do have great luck with cedars." He gave me a scornful look and answered, "Luck, indeed! I give the most minute attention when digging up the trees to preserve the roots intact, to make the hole to receive the tree large enough, to have the earth fine and free from stones, and then closely packed in about the roots after the tree is set, to have the stones properly placed, to keep the tree firm and the roots moist,— do you call all this luck? " Of course there was no reply whatever from me.

It may not be generally known that most of the box edging sold by dealers in this country is imported from Europe, every year, in the early spring. Much of it comes from France, and none of it seems to be able to resist our changeable winter climate. After losing large quantities of box edging every winter for years, I have discovered a way of preserving it through our constantly rising and falling temperatures.

Late in November, the ground over the roots receives a good mulch of cow manure, then stakes about two feet long are driven at alternate intervals of three feet on each side of the edging, boards are then placed on edge so that they lean against these stakes, meeting at the top like an "A." The box is thus protected from the sun, which, shining upon the frozen foliage, is what causes most of it to die. I believe that box edging, when thus protected, could be grown in localities where it has heretofore been thought impossible.

Every four years, about the middle of April, it is well to take up all the box edging, trench the ground where it is to be reset, and replant it. The object of this is to keep the box bushy, and prevent it from growing " leggy," or showing a wood stem below with a bunch of green at the top, as frequently happens. It is not well to take up at a time more plants than one can replant the same day; they should be reset just touching each other, and it will be found that there is always a considerable number of plants left over, which, if the garden is of any size, will be welcomed with joy. This process has been successfully followed, not far from my own place, in a small formal garden, where the box is now over seventy-five years old, and remains always thick and beautiful.

The quantity of box edging can be easily increased by taking off clippings every year except the year it is reset. These clippings, made of little branches three to four inches long, may be taken in June after the box has made its first growth, and either set in rows in a bed prepared for them or planted at once where they are to grow, as edging surrounding beds or borders. I have done this with great success, but it is a waste of time and material unless the clippings are thoroughly wet at least once a day, and twice a day if the weather is very hot or dry.

If any one has a friend in whose garden old box is growing, let her beg clippings from it, for it will be more likely to prove hardy than the box one buys.

Every year, in August, the box edging can be clipped; and, if it grows where winter covering is necessary, it should not be allowed to reach more than a foot in height.

All of us have noticed, at the end of the winter, the sad-looking box trees and bushes on the steps and windows of the houses on the north sides of the streets in New York, also on the sides of the avenues where the sun shines upon it, by the end of March there is rarely a green bush to be seen, whereas on the south side of the streets, where the bushes are protected from the sun, they are quite likely to live.

Sheared plants of American arborvitæ would answer the purpose of supplying an evergreen exterior decoration, and, unless neglected or allowed to become too dry or root-bound, will live for several years, even under the abnormal conditions of life they find in the city.

Upon every place, even those where space is limited, a few evergreens should be grown, even if only one pine, one hemlock and one spruce, with a few of the smaller varieties of evergreens. To people who spend any time in the late autumn or during the winter in the country, the evergreens will give extreme delight. Even if the country house is closed during all the cold months, the evergreens should still be grown, not only for the beauty they add to the place,—as a house in winter-time looks cold and lonely with nothing green

The hill country in which lies the garden

near it,—but also for the value they give to deciduous trees and shrubs in spring and summer.

Small, choice evergreens about a place, such as the finer arborvitæ, retinisporas, and other Japanese evergreens, and even the native cedars and hemlocks, are wonderfully improved by an annual clipping in August of each year. This clipping need not be more than an inch, or at the most two inches, but it has great effect in thickening and beautifying the foliage. There is no comparison in beauty between a tree that has been clipped for three successive years and one that has never been clipped. This treatment is especially necessary to the evergreens in formal gardens, for by this means the trees may be kept at the height and size desired. Unclipped trees will usually be open and ragged looking, while those that have been clipped will have very much finer and almost impenetrable foliage.

The native cedars, of which there are several varieties, among them one almost as blue as the *Retinispora squarrosa*, can give us all the formal effect that we may desire in our gardens; these cedars respond to the yearly clipping with great thickness of foliage.

It is very interesting to sit in the garden when this operation is being carried on. One may have a book or sewing in her hands, but it is so fascinating to watch the outline of the tree gradually coming out sharply from the work of the shears that little sewing or reading is done at such times.

Few of the evergreens will live in my soil, hemlocks and red cedars being the only members of the family that really do well.

The white pine, American arborvitæ and the spruce struggle along for a time, protesting against the conditions of life as they find it; but the retinisporas, yews, all the finer evergreens, notwithstanding specially prepared soil and winter covering, do not long survive. My garden at Meadowburn is situated in the extreme northerly corner of the beautiful hill country of northern New Jersey and New York, directly on the boundary line of the two states. The winter temperature rises and falls from forty degrees above zero to ten, and often twenty degrees below, and in summer, during July and August, there is usually a long period of dry weather, which make conditions that are especially hard upon the finer evergreen family.

The great hemlocks, the symmetrical spruces, the solemn pines, which in a natural state grow near the white birches so often that one might say the pines are married to the birches—indeed, all evergreens—inspire me with a feeling almost akin to worship, possibly a heathen trait which has survived generations of civilization, so that it is a great trial to me not to be able to grow the evergreen family successfully.

As a compensation, I was able to plan for a friend a most lovely little garden which she calls her " evergreen garden." It occupies the basement area from which an old side-hill barn had been removed. The space is only about forty-five by sixty feet. Across the back of the garden is a wall of rough stone about eight feet high, once the back foundation wall of the barn. In the crevices of the stones are planted ferns, ivy is trained against them, and in the center, from a simple wall fountain, water drips with musical sound into a basin below.

High grass banks rise on the two sides of the garden, and the front opens upon a beautiful lawn, bordered with old trees and sloping to the water. Steps of natural rough stone lead down from the summit of one of the grassy banks into the little garden; around three sides, and in several formal beds set in turf are planted many varieties of small and rare evergreens. All are surrounded with box edging, and had one not seen a like collection of evergreens it would be impossible to imagine there could be such variety of form and shade from darkest to lightest green, including the beautiful blue-greens, golden yellow and green tipped with yellow.

Although natives of many countries, all the specimens have lived and thriven in the sandy soil and moist air of their new home by the sea; and the little evergreen garden, both summer and winter, is a joy to all who behold it.

RAISING FLOWERS FROM SEED

CHAPTER III

ONE of the greatest pleasures to the gardener is in raising flowers, both perennials and annuals, from seed; and especially is it interesting to gather and sow the seeds saved from her own finest plants. I always mark the plants whose seeds I wish to save by tying white strings about the stems when in full bloom as a sign to all that that blossom must not be cut. My maid keeps me supplied with a box containing little pieces, about eight inches long and an inch wide, of white muslin, black cambric, pink cambric and turkey-red. I tie black upon the plants that are to be cast out in the autumn; scarlet upon the very bright red phloxes; a pink and white string upon all those of pink and white varieties; and a single white piece upon the

71

choice white phloxes, and also upon all plants whose seeds I wish to save.

The seeds, after maturing, are gathered when dry, put into boxes, each of which is carefully labeled, and then sown either in August or the following spring.

The seeds of perennials take longer to germinate than those of annuals, and often, when one has abandoned all hope of their coming up, they will at last appear. One year, some platycodons sown in my garden in August did not show signs of life until the middle of the following May; so one must be patient and give Nature her own time. When there is much rain in April and May before the seeds sown in the seed-beds have germinated, the smaller varieties are quite apt to rot in the ground, and I have lost many a crop of Canterbury bells from this cause. Seeds more often fail to come up because of too wet weather after sowing, or because they have been allowed to become too dry, or because they have been planted too deep, than through any fault of the seedsman's seeds. At first, when beginning gardening, I laid upon the seedsman all the blame for any failure of the seeds to germinate, but now I know that such is rarely the case. It is either unfavorable weather conditions or carelessness on the part of the gardener. If, when the little germ is about to break through the enclosing husk, it is allowed to become dry for twenty-four hours, it will be killed; while, on the other hand, too much water at this time will also cause it to die.

Children are generally taught to make their gardens with annuals, but it will be very interesting to the little ones if taught to plant the seeds of the perennials in the spring, to watch them growing through the summer, to separate them into rows in July and then in the autumn to transplant them again to the places where they are to grow. On coming back the next year, their interest will be further aroused when they find the little plants growing sturdily along, and then see them year after year becoming more beautiful, and finally giving up their seeds in turn to raise other plants for the garden, or to be given away to friends.

Delphinium. After the phlox, so precious to us all, it is difficult to say which of the hardy perennials is most valuable; but, first among them must come the delphinium, or larkspur. No other perennial grows so luxuriantly, none is more easy to raise from seed, and the great variety of shades of blue, the height of the plants and the length of their spikes of bloom—many being two feet and over in length—unite to make this plant unique. The majority of the larkspurs in my garden last summer reached the height of six feet, and many were, by actual measurement, over eight feet high. Then, of course, there were also the smaller-growing varieties from three to four feet high.

The number of varieties of delphinium is infinite. Kelway, of Langport, Somerset,

England, the greatest specialist in these plants, lists two hundred and thirty-four varieties, and asks for some as high as 10s. 10d. apiece, and £18 for a choice set of two dozen. He also asks five shillings a packet for the seeds. These prices are far above those asked by growers in the United States, many of whom have obtained their seeds from Kelway in the first instance, and the Gold Medal hybrids sold in this country give a sufficient variety. Of the delphiniums, the dark blue splashed with purple, the light blue with lavender whose individual double flowers are as large as the blossom of a stock, the light blue flushed with pink, the pale blue with a white center, the turquoise and the sky-blue are among the most beautiful.

On October 10th, from a third crop of blossoms, I counted fourteen varieties; and in the first week in September, 1909, I was able to take the first prize at the county fair with flowers from plants raised from seed sown in the open ground, just one year before, and grown entirely out-of-doors. The professional gardeners at the fair asked my men many questions as to how we had raised such fine flowers. Afterward, when I inquired if they had told everything we did, they replied, "No, or they might beat us next year."

The seeds of delphinium may be sown in the open as soon as the ground is warm in spring, by the end of July the little plants may be set out six inches apart and moved again to their final dwelling-place October 1st, or early the following spring. I have met with the greatest success, however, in sowing seeds saved from particularly beautiful lark-spurs in the empty seed-bed about the end of August, covering the crowns of the plants with coal-ashes in autumn, and strewing a little straw or coarse hay over them for the first winter. The following year, when the seed-beds are needed for the annuals, the little plants are transplanted in rows one foot apart into a nursery bed, where they bloom during the first summer. By October 1st

A CLUMP OF DELPHINUMS

their permanent home is prepared and there they are carefully removed.

If some of the delphiniums are to be placed in the back of a border, they are planted two feet apart, as in the borders we want the growth to be close; but, if they are to be grown in rows, these rows are made three feet apart and trenched one foot deep. In the bottom of the trench about seven inches of cow manure is placed, and the trench is filled high with rich earth because it will always settle; the plants, then one year old, are set out three feet apart in the trench, and in the late autumn some coal-ashes are sifted over them. In two years' time rows so planted are a solid mass of color when the larkspurs are blooming.

In the spring, when the plants are well up, a large trowelful of bone meal is dug about each plant, and when they are three feet in height they are all staked. This is absolutely necessary because of the winds, as the stalks of the delphinium are so tender that one

THE PRACTICAL FLOWER GARDEN

heavy blow would make havoc among them; so when they are about three feet in height we always stake them.

August 1st a little nitrate of soda is dug about them and carefully watered in; they then receive a mulch of clippings of lawn grass or leaves from the year before and are again watered freely, and the more they are watered the more they will respond with bloom.

If a stalk is cut down as soon as the flowers are withered, the plant will immediately begin to send up another, and in this way one is able to have a constant succession of bloom. I always have at least three crops of flowers from the delphinium, but only the stalks of the first crop will reach any great height.

The delphiniums do not care to be moved after they are eighteen months old. It is possible, of course, but the plants do not thrive as well when moved after they are so old, and it is better to allow them to remain wherever they may be than to take the risk of moving such large plants. There are many ten-year-old larskpurs in my garden which send up from eighteen to twenty spikes of bloom at the same time. Last summer a number bore over thirty stalks at the first blooming.

The coal-ashes sifted over the crowns of the delphinium in the spring and fall are absolutely necessary to preserve them from their fatal enemy, the white grub. One of my friends said: "I do not care for delphiniums because I do not like to see the place where they grow look like a cinder-bed." But the cinder effect will be avoided if the ashes are finely sifted.

The roots of the delphiniums should not be allowed to come in contact with manure. I believe that manure, if allowed to touch the roots, is as fatal to the delphinium as it is to the lily bulb.

Pyrethrum is another perennial that has been greatly improved of late years. Many varieties are listed by growers in this country, and Kelway advertises two hundred and eighteen varieties. They come in all shades, from palest pink to dark crimson, also white, lavender and purple. They are single-, double- and anemone-flowered. They bloom from the end of May through June, when they should be cut down. If they are then fed with bone meal, they will bloom again in September. The seeds can be sown and the plants grown just as are the larkspurs, for they germinate readily and are equally hardy. They are also subject to attacks by the same white grub which is the enemy of the larkspur, and should have the coal-ashes sprinkled over them, as is done for the larkspurs.

Starwort. Another great perennial family is the starwort, or hardy aster, or Michælmas daisy, as they are sometimes called in their natural state. These are the wild asters which clothe the hillsides, roadsides, and fence-rows with beauty in the autumn. But the hybridizer has wrought his magic upon them, and a hundred and twenty-nine varieties are now listed by Kelway.

In color the starworts range from white through shades of palest lavender and amethyst to deep purple, and through shades of pale pink to dark rose. They are easily raised from seed sown in the spring and, if transplanted in the autumn where they are to live, will bloom the following year. They grow from two to four feet in height and, if raised in both early and late varieties, will bloom from the end of July until well into November. Their natural place is in masses in the shrubberies, planted among evergreens, or in large, mixed, herbaceous borders.

Anchusa Italica. A perennial not yet very much grown, but which when once known will always find a place in the garden, is the *Anchusa Italica,* or Italian Alkanet, Dropmore variety. Two-year-old plants in my garden were seven feet high in June, and were continually covered for six weeks with small blue flowers formed in clusters eighteen inches long. The seeds may be sown in August as soon as they are dry, and in late autumn the little plants should be covered with some stable litter.

The *Anchusa Italica* also seeds itself, and by October 1st a number of young plants will always be growing about their parent.

Marguerite carnations are so valuable that every one should give a little space to these flowers. The seeds can be sown as soon as the ground is warm in the spring, and in June the little plants can be separated into rows about a foot apart and will begin to bloom August 1st. They require a rich soil and plenty of water. They come in every color and shade, and their blossoms are at least two and a half inches in diameter; the stems are long and they flower until ice forms. People, on seeing a bowl of them in the house in mid-summer, have often remarked: "Why there are hot-house carnations!"

Late in the autumn, the tops should be cut down and the plants covered over with stable litter. They will then bloom again the second year. Occasionally they will bloom a third year, but for the third year they cannot be relied upon, so if one would have them in the garden, a sowing of seed should be made every other year.

Pentstemons are another group of perennials which come in a number of colors,—white, pink, crimson, scarlet, purple and magenta. The different varieties bloom from June through September and can be grown from seed sown in the spring; the roots may also be separated, as is done with the phloxes. A little bone meal given them in May of the second year will stimulate their growth. They are all hardy excepting one variety, Sensation, the freest bloomer of all, which should be lifted and placed in a coldframe for the winter.

Salvia azurea grandiflora is another flower lately brought forward by growers. Each stalk ends in a large, loose cluster of pale blue flowers which lasts for five or six weeks. The plant grows about three feet high; it can be raised from seed sown at the same time as other perennials, and is grateful for the addition of sand to the soil, which need be only that of the well-made border. Though a native of the Rocky mountains, it needs a winter protection of stable litter or leaves, and the young plants will be the better for spending the first winter in a coldframe. The *Salvia azurea* may also be increased by dividing large roots. Since knowing this plant, I do not feel that I could be quite happy without it.

Hyacinthus candicans is a flower not sufficiently grown. It has great merits of hardiness, and in decorative qualities. It is also inexpensive when bought in quantity and is easily raised from seed. It grows from a bulb, and is most effective when planted in clumps of from six to a dozen or more together. It blooms in August, throwing up a great spike of white blossoms at least four feet in height, and looks like a magnificent hyacinth.

Monkshood. In every garden there should be a corner for the monkshood, as it blooms at a time when there are only a few flowers left to us. I have often gathered it after thick ice had formed. The plants remain in blossom on the stalk a long time, and in the house will keep fresh in water for ten days. One should have not only the dark blue variety, but also the new Wilsoni recently imported from China. The roots may be separated, but they are easily grown from seed, like other perennials, and need only good soil of the borders.

Peony. It is not generally known how simple it is to grow both the iris and peonies from seed. This is especially interesting when we have a beautiful variety of which we do not know the name, and are therefore unable to order more like it. By the process of raising

85

the plants from seed we may increase our stock indefinitely. We mark the plants whose seeds we wish to save, gather the peony seed when it is ripe, which should be about the end of August, and sow it at once in drills in rich soil. The places where the peony seeds are sown should be marked by stakes because the seeds will not germinate until the following May. The little plants must be kept free from weeds and watered, and the second year separated a foot or so apart in rows; the third year the peonies will generally bloom.

Iris. The iris seeds should be gathered when ripe and sown the following April in drills like pea seed, then transplanted when three or four inches high; if they have had rich soil and all the water they need, they will frequently blossom the second summer. Last year I raised about three hundred plants in this manner.

There are so many annuals that it is difficult to know which to speak about; however,

Asters following Iris and Lilies

a few are chosen because of their luxuriant growth or for the color they give us.

The first of these is the *Amaranthus Abyssinicus*. This plant has a very Oriental-Arabian-Nights sounding name, and rivals Jack's bean-stalk in growth, for it reaches a height of seven or eight feet in a short time. The stalk and branches are dark crimson in color, and every branch terminates with a cluster of dark crimson tassels a foot in length; it has a very large light green leaf.

One of these plants appeared one summer in my seed-beds. I did not know what it was. It grew and grew, and finally one of the gardeners, a man along in life, who was trained by my grandmother's gardener, pronounced it the "lady's riding whip," a name which had probably been given it from the long tassel effect, and at last I was able to trace it in the catalogues. It is very effective when grown either in the back of an herbaceous border or in a shrubbery.

Nicotiana, both Sylvestris, Affinis and the hybrid varieties which yield larger flowers than the ordinary tobacco plant and range through many colors, are very simply raised from seed, and, as they bloom continuously, are a great addition to our gardens.

A charming, old-time annual is the *kochia,* or summer cypress. It seeds itself, so that if there is even one plant in the garden seed need never be bought. When the little plants are a couple of inches in height they should be transplanted to a foot apart. They grow two feet high, are naturally symmetrical in growth, have pale green, feathery foliage, and make a charming little hedge about the seed-bed or the nursery. In autumn the foliage turns dark crimson.

Salpiglossis is a valuable annual, blooming so luxuriantly that one wonders that any plant can produce so many blossoms. The flowers are white splotched with crimson, or pink flushed with white, lilac and purple. It only grows about a foot in height, but gives a constant amount of color.

Schizanthus, or butterfly-flower, is an annual well worth growing. It comes in many colors and is continually covered with flowers, white, pink and lilac. When three or more are grown in a large pot, it makes a handsome decoration for the terrace.

The old-fashioned *Phlox Drummondi* has been greatly improved and is now a very effective annual, not only for color in the garden, but also as a household decoration. The *Phlox Drummondi* does very well when sown directly where it is to bloom.

All of these annuals need only to be sown in rows in the seed-bed as soon as the ground is warm in the spring, watered late in the day, and when the plants are about three inches high transplanted where it is intended that they shall bloom.

There are a few annuals which should be sown in the hotbed by March 1st if we wish them to come into bloom early. They may also be sown in the open ground, but in that case their flowers are very late and only reach their perfection with the coming of cold weather. The most important of these are *stocks* and *snapdragons*. If, when the little plants are set out in the open ground in May, they show a tendency to become stringy and form only a few buds at the end of the stalk, they should promptly be cut down. One need not be alarmed at this process because almost instantly the plant will send up a new and sturdy growth. This weakness of the plants results because either they were grown too thickly in the hotbed or did not receive sufficient air.

Heliotrope and *ageratum* are two other annuals necessary in the garden because of their color and prolific flowering. Ageratum is of all blue flowers the freest bloomer. It is also easy to raise and every seed seems to germ-

A tangled corner

inate. But the heliotrope is more difficult to
start, and unless the gardener is experienced
he should procure slips, and start them in
February in fine, sharp sand, transferring the
little plants when well rooted to thumb-pots,
and again to three-inch pots early in April.
The heliotrope requires more heat than the
hotbeds yield, and the slips must be grown
either in a greenhouse or in a window of a
rather warm living-room.

Verbenas germinate readily, and seeds sown
in the hotbeds in March will be fine plants by
the end of May, when it is time to set them
out.

All the single *dahlias*, too, are easily raised
from seed sown in the hotbeds about March
1st, and when so started the period of bloom
is greatly increased. By the early start thus
obtained the dahlias raised from seed are
particularly fine in form and color. Dormant
tubers of double dahlias can be started about
April 1st in a coldframe.

Then there are the *petunias*, Rosy Morn, Giant Ruffled White, and all the other ruffled varieties. It is a simple matter to raise them from seed; many varieties yield a plant from every seed in the ordinary packet, while of other varieties from twenty-five to seventy-five plants are grown from a single packet of seed.

In the hotbeds, over the horse manure which provides the heat necessary for forcing, we use a soil composed of old sods, leaf-mold, very fine old, cow manure, sand and some garden soil. This preparation is also used in the flats and pots in which the young plants are grown; the same soil is used in the coldframes.

If fine, dry sea sand is thinly sifted over the seeds when planted and they are then gently pressed down by the hand, they will retain the moisture better; the young plants seem also less apt to "damp off" than when covered with soil.

The durable quality of concrete and the

AN ENTRANCE INTO THE FORMAL GARDEN

protection it affords from low temperatures as well as from moles and field-mice warrant its use for coldframes and hotbeds. The construction is simple, and two men who understand mixing concrete and constructing the frames can excavate the earth and make half a dozen frames in a week.

The so-called "Sunlight Sash," a recently patented sash for hotbeds and coldframes, which consists of double sash with an air space of three-quarters of an inch between the layers of glass, seems to be an improvement over the single glass. It permits the sash to remain uncovered and open to the sun and light in all but very severe weather. Because of the increase of warmth and the amount of light received, there seems to be less danger from mildew, the plants grow larger and stronger and many flowers can be kept blooming all winter, and lettuce and radishes can more easily be raised in successive crops during the cold months, than in the old way.

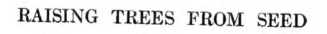

RAISING TREES FROM SEED

CHAPTER IV

RAISING TREES FROM SEED

UNTIL recent years, people in this country have wholly failed to appreciate the importance of tree and forest culture. Our natural forests have been abundant, timber and forest products have been plentiful and cheap, and we have gone on oblivious to our future needs, recklessly wasting or negligently unconcerned about our timber and forest resources. We have been, both individually and as a people, wholly indifferent to the priceless value of our woodlands and forests as equalizers of temperature, or as conservators of our springs, brooks and water sources, or even as mere wood and lumber.

The lumberman has cut wastefully, with no other object than the price of his product in the open market, and fires have everywhere

97

followed the lumberman's brush, rubbish and waste, with the final result of leaving many of our former woodlands and forests treeless wastes of blackened stumps and ground.

Now there has come a change of heart, and we hear constantly of conservation of natural resources, of forest planting and protection, of the protection of woodlands and trees,— and the call comes none too soon for the future welfare of all concerned.

In response to this call, the forestry division of the United States Department of Agriculture has done, and is doing, a great work both in planting and preserving the forests and in instructing people through pamphlets and circulars issued by it how to re-forest and protect their woodlands. Its plans are wise and far-reaching, but its energies are limited by the appropriations allowed by Congress.

Every intelligent person should coöperate with the government, and endeavor to do something every year toward educating the people to a greater appreciation of the importance of replanting and preserving forests and woodlands. Arbor Day is a step forward, but all children should be taught to know the trees and to love them. This is quite possible even in cities because of the fine parks where many varieties of trees are growing. In spring and summer, classes might be held in the parks after school hours, which would be of invaluable benefit in acquainting the children with the different species of trees, their several characteristics and uses, the importance of preserving them, as well as the manner of planting a tree whenever there is space and opportunity.

For the last three years there has been serious drought in many sections and during this time in my own part of the country, where usually ground-water is abundant, the springs and streams have rarely attained their levels. This increasing condition of persistent drought should be a warning of the disaster which may overtake us if we do not learn in time to renew and preserve our woodlands and forests, which are so essential for the proper conservation of our water supplies.

I often regret that I did not long ago, during all the years spent in raising other things, begin also to raise trees from seeds. Sturdy groves of timber might now be growing from seeds sown twenty-five years ago.

All those who own suburban or country property should keep it well planted and preserved as a duty to future generations who are to inherit the land.

All young married people beginning life in the country should start at once to raise trees if their place is of any extent. By middle life, when grandchildren come, the trees will not only be splendid specimens, but will be monuments to the ancestral forethought and love of beauty; and because they were planted by some forbear will be regarded with increased tenderness and devotion as long as their great branches spread themselves in air.

It is not generally understood that the conifers, both the white and red pine, the Scotch pine and the native hemlocks, can easily be raised from seed, which, though a slow process, is one most interesting, as well as quite simple, and well worth trying where the estate is of any size. Cones may be gathered in September and spread upon a sheet in a light room of a tool house or other dry place where they will dry; the seeds will fall out from the cones and can then be collected and stored through the winter in boxes, or the seeds may be bought in the spring from any reliable seedsman. The seed-bed should be made in the same way as are the seed-beds for flowers: it should be raised about four inches above the surface of the ground, to secure perfect drainage; a good size is four by six feet. At the four corners of the bed, stout stakes, eighteen inches high, should be driven into the ground, and a board a foot in width running around the bed nailed to the stakes. When the ground is warm, about the time that we would plant beans in the vegetable garden, the ground should be thoroughly moistened to the depth of several inches, and the seed sown thickly in drills about four inches apart; then the seed should be pressed well into the soil with the flat surface of the hoe and about an eighth of an inch of soil sprinkled over the whole bed. Over the bed and resting upon the tops of the four stakes a screen made of lath should be laid, to protect the young seedlings from the too strong sun of the summer. In natural conditions where the conifers seed themselves, they are protected by the pine needles and by the leaves, the underbrush and the tall trees above them; hence, when raising them in the nursery, we should give them as nearly as possible the conditions that they would naturally have.

The first year, the little plants need no other care than to be kept free from weeds and not allowed to become too dry. After very heavy rains the lath screen may be lifted for a day to enable the bed to dry out. In about three weeks after sowing the seed the little plants begin to appear above the earth, and at the end of the first summer should be about two and one-half inches high. This seems a far cry to the pine tree towering fifty feet in the air, but we do not plant such trees for ourselves, but for our children; still a pine tree should be fifty feet high in less than fifty years.

Two ounces of seed will sow a bed four by six feet, and allowing for seeds that do not germinate and for young plants that die in the first four years of life (they will rarely die after four years), should raise five hundred trees; and one pound of seed, after making a large allowance for those that do not germinate and for trees that do not live, should raise four thousand trees.

With the first frost in the autumn, the lath screen may be removed from the seed-bed which, toward the end of November of the first year, may then be covered with a spread of fallen leaves, and the whole protected by a single thickness of burlap nailed over the entire bed where the young plants are growing. This is to give them for the first year the necessary winter protection, as in the forest they would have the natural protection of the fallen leaves and pine needles.

During the second summer the little plants remain in the seed-bed and need no care except to be kept free from weeds and occasionally watered if they become too dry. They do not need the lath screen nor any further covering in the second winter.

The third year they should be transplanted; trenches of good, rich earth should be made in the nursery a foot apart, and the little trees very carefully lifted from the seed-bed with a spade, put first into a pail of liquid mud, so that the roots do not become dry, and then set out about eight inches apart in rows in the nursery. Here, again, they need no care except to be kept free from weeds and occasionally watered.

The fourth summer, they may either be transplanted to their permanent place or be

ENTRANCE TO THE CEDAR WALK

reset to twelve or fourteen inches apart in the nursery.

The object of this frequent transplanting is to cause the young trees to make fibrous root-growth. If we dig up a little pine tree or hemlock in the woods, it will be found to have a tap-root and two or three side roots; whereas, the nursery-grown tree is composed of a mass of fibrous roots, and these fibrous roots enable the tree to stand the transplanting and to make a quick growth, so that our four-year-old tree grown in the nursery has great vitality of root and is almost sure to live.

The United States Forestry Department recommends the planting of pine trees at a distance of six feet apart in all directions. This is, of course, for those who are growing pines for lumber; but on a private estate, where one does not grow them with any intention of cutting them down in a few years, to sell, they would naturally be placed with an idea of beauty in the landscape.

Pine trees will grow anywhere, on almost

any kind of soil except in low places; one never sees pine trees growing in damp meadows or wet places.

If one wishes to make a hedge of white pine the ground should be trenched in the same way as it is for any other hedge, and the young plants then set out, two feet apart. They will grow rapidly, and in a short time will form a hedge five or six feet in height and three or four feet wide at the base, and be an object of the greatest beauty. It needs trimming but once a year, and in color and foliage makes a hedge surpassing in beauty that of any other evergreen. Such hedges of white pine are seen in perfection at Cornish, N. H., where one particularly fine surrounds the place of the late Mr. St. Gaudens.

One of the few hard-wood trees which has not yet, in our part of the country, been attacked by any enemy is the black walnut. These trees are rapid in growth, and very graceful in form; the foliage is sufficiently light to permit of the grass growing under the

trees well up to the trunk and the shape of
the trunk and the limbs is so fine in the winter-
time that there is no tree better worth planting about any estate where it will grow than
the black walnut. The lumber and wood are
in great demand and, raised in quantities, and
cut judiciously, are a valuable asset for the
farmer.

Some fifteen years ago a young seedling
black walnut appeared in one of my seed-beds.
The nut had probably been dropped there by
some squirrel. It grew nearly two feet the
first year, and as a matter of curiosity we
allowed the sapling to remain, but it grew so
rapidly that in a couple of years it became
necessary to remove it from the seed-bed.
The tree is now about twenty inches in cir-
cumference and has reached a height of over
thirty feet, which is doing well for fifteen
years' growth.

If, along in October, one gathers a bag of
walnuts, removes the green shells, and, going
about the place, makes here and there a hole

in the ground, some two or three inches deep, with a pointed stick or crowbar, drops in a nut, and presses the soil down with his foot, the next year he will have a vigorous shoot; the following year the tree will begin to grow, and in an astonishingly short time whoever has followed this practice will be rewarded by a fine lot of young black walnut trees upon his place. One could easily gather up and plant a bagful of nuts in a forenoon. Perhaps the best places for planting are along fence-rows, which afford the tree in its first tender years some protection from drought and severe winters, as well as as from interference by cattle.

It is almost impossible to transplant a field-grown black walnut and get it to live, so that one gets the best results by planting the nuts where the tree is to remain.

Another symmetrical and beautiful tree, also of rapid growth and free from attacks of borers and insects, is the ash. Two seedling ash trees, also found in my seed-bed, were transplanted when a year old, and eighteen inches high, and after fifteen years' growth the trees were about as large as the black walnut seedling, but a year ago, as they were crowding more valuable trees, they had to be cut down.

The linden tree and the sycamore are also healthy, of rapid growth, and are not difficult to raise from seed.

The maple needs no brief to tell of its merits, but should not be planted near house or garden because of its dense shade.

In tracts of woodland, under maples, about the parent sweet gum tree, near sycamores, ashes, birches, lindens, many wild seedlings will be found, and these, if carefully lifted in the early spring, transplanted to the nursery and there cultivated for a year or two, will make fine, strong trees. The finest seedlings are to be found on low ground or along the banks of streams, where there is moisture and protection of undergrowth from too strong sun. We have but to study natural conditions and try to reproduce or to improve upon them to be successful in raising our trees from seeds.

The *Catalpa speciosa* also seeds itself readily, and, wherever a parent tree grows near a shrubbery or spot where the grass is not mown, there one can find every year a few young trees ready to be transplanted early in the spring. No tree is more decorative than the catalpa with its beautiful leaves and panicles of orchid-like flowers. It also lives to great age, and its twisted, gnarled trunks and branches rival in beauty those of the old apple tree.

Nature sows her seeds when ripened, and the seeds of maple, birch and elm ripen and fall to the ground between April and June; they should then be gathered and planted without delay as they retain their vitality for a short time only—perhaps six weeks. They germinate soon after planting.

The germ of life in the seeds of all nut-bearing trees survives but a season, and hence the nuts should be planted in the autumn as soon as ripe and dry.

Willows are best grown from cuttings made early in March or April, from eight to twelve inches long. They grow so rapidly that they may be planted where they are to grow. Straight branches of willow, five or six feet high, if cut in March and planted in a moist place, will generally grow, but must, of course, be staked. They need only to be thrust about a foot into the ground.

The yellow poplar is easily grown from cuttings a foot in length, taken in March or April, and planted four inches deep and about the same distance apart, in a shallow trench of good soil. All cuttings of trees should be kept moist and shaded from the sun until well rooted, and generally treated the same as the cuttings from shrubs. Early the following spring they may be transplanted to the places where they are to grow.

Lombardy poplars send up shoots from the roots, which may be severed from the root by a sharp spade, and planted early in the spring where they are to grow. They should be kept staked for a couple of years. Every year we separate these shoots from the poplar trees in the garden, sometimes keeping them in rows for a year, and again planting them at once in permanent places. By degrees we are planting these poplars wherever there is space, just inside the stone walls that border the roadway, almost too unfrequented to be called a highway, that runs through the farm. Of more than a hundred of these little shoots thus planted not one has died, although several have been broken by cattle, which eat the poplar leaves with avidity.

The deciduous-tree seeds that germinate most easily are maple, catalpa, ash, linden, birch, oak, walnut, and hickory. Of the seeds of the tulip tree but a small proportion—from five to ten per cent—germinate; it is a tree difficult to raise from seed.

The seed-bed for seeds of deciduous trees should be prepared in the same manner as for evergreens. The seeds should be sown in rows from eight to twelve inches apart; light seeds such as those of birch, elm, catalpa and maples, should be spaced about two inches apart in the row so that the seedlings will not require thinning. A day when there is no wind should be chosen for sowing these seeds, or many will be blown away and the sower's patience be sorely tried. After sowing cover the seeds lightly about twice their own depth, pressing down the earth firmly with the back of the hoe; sprinkle the bed, and scatter over it a covering of any kind of chaff which will preserve the moisture in the soil for some time; when watering is necessary, the chaff serves as a filter, and also as a preventive against washing the little seeds out of the soil. A very fine spray should always be used for watering tree seeds. When the seedlings appear the chaff should be removed. The bed must be kept carefully weeded and gently cultivated between the rows, particularly in dry weather, and during the first winter it should be protected with a covering of leaves about a foot in depth.

During the first year in the seed-bed, ash seedlings should grow from eight to ten inches; elm, eight to ten; black locust, eight to twenty; locust, eight to twelve; oak, eight to twelve; birch, four to six; maple, ten to twelve; catalpa, eighteen to twenty inches.

Early spring is the best time for transplanting the seedlings, which should be first lifted into a pail of thin mud, the roots well covered with the mud, and then planted carefully, the roots being given ample room; the earth should be firmly packed about them, and a mulch of old manure or leaves laid around them and, if possible, watered from time to time.

Maples, catalpas and locusts make such rapid growth that after a year in the seedbed they may be transplanted to the place where they are to grow. Other varieties are benefited by being first transplanted to rows in the nursery for a year, and there cultivated by the hoe before being finally transplanted. All the seeds of nut trees, acorns,

Meadow–burn

walnuts and hickories, should be planted in the autumn, preferably where they are to grow.

The ravages of the chestnut borer have made it undesirable to raise this beautiful tree at present.

Seeds of locusts, sycamores and catalpas should be gathered when ripe, then mixed with dry sand and stored in a cool, dry cellar until spring. Locust seeds, before planting, should be placed in a vessel of very hot water, stirred for a few minutes, and then allowed to soak in the water (which of course will become cold) for three days; then taken out and planted at once, not being allowed to become dry.

It would be of the greatest benefit to the country if the owners of land everywhere would plant trees intelligently and extensively. By this means, the abandoned farm could be made productive, shelter and wind-breaks provided for buildings and pastures, covert for game and song birds and protection for growing crops. The necessary wood for fuel, building repairs, and fence-making, could also be produced cheaply, and the whole country made more beautiful. It is not difficult to grow the trees needed for this planting, and the sowing of the seeds, their transplanting and winter protection are quite similar to the care necessary in raising perennials from seed, infinitely more interesting, and require only a small corner of the vegetable garden for seed-beds and nursery.

A little seed-bed, four feet by six feet, and a couple of rows twenty feet long for a nursery where the seedlings could be transplanted to live for a year or two, is all the space required to raise many trees—enough at least to fully plant a place of ten acres, as well as to furnish an occupation and a delightful source of interest to all the members of a family.

May the present lively interest in tree planting and forest culture continue and increase, until everywhere our waste lands and denuded hills are again covered with growing timber with all its beauty of form and coloring.

FERTILIZERS AND HOW TO APPLY THEM, TOGETHER WITH SOME PLANT REMEDIES

CHAPTER V

FERTILIZERS AND HOW TO APPLY THEM,
TOGETHER WITH SOME PLANT REMEDIES

FORMERLY, the feeding of infants was a comparatively simple matter. They were given milk, and, after the first few months, a cereal; but today the nourishment of young children has become serious and intricate, and the food of each child is prepared according to a special prescription, moderated thus and so from " milk from the top of the bottle ;" one cannot wonder if the hair of grandmothers left in charge of their children's children becomes prematurely white in consequence.

In former times, the gardener used only manure, or if he were quite advanced in his craft, some bone meal, as stimulants for his flowers. Fertilizers, today, are as many in number as the prescriptions for infants' foods, and, in the seedsmen's catalogues, many different varieties are listed for the various fruits, for vegetables, and for the flower garden. Not all are necessary, but some knowledge of the different requirements of the various flowers, of the food best suited to each plant with which it will achieve the best results, is one of the most interesting studies of the modern gardener.

Among our friends, there are some who cannot eat red meats, uncooked fruits, salads, or other foods. The fact is accepted without comment, and the hostess provides such articles of diet for her guests as are best suited to their conditions. Why, therefore, should not the plants that reward us with such luxuriant bloom for the care bestowed upon them receive each the nourishment upon which it thrives the best? Chief and best of all for grass, vegetable and flower gardens, is cow manure which should be at least five or six months old before it is used; fresh and finely ground bone meal is invaluable for roses, young trees, and many flowers; poudrette, a preparation of native guano, sold by Dreer of Philadelphia, is a clean, odorless fertilizer, rich in ammonia, and excellent for many perennials especially the phlox.

Soot, which may be bought by the bushel or taken from the chimneys, is the best possible nutriment for bay trees and box, and, when mixed with equal portions of sulphur and dusted upon plants in an incipient stage of mildew, will cause its immediate arrest.

Bon Arbor, a commercial fertilizer recently placed upon the market, has a wonderful effect upon dahlias, heliotrope, petunias and many annuals. This is an expensive fertilizer, costing thirty dollars a hundred pounds, but a little goes a long way, as one pound is dissolved in thirty gallons of water, and the dose consists of half a pint of the solution poured slowly on the ground directly over the roots of the plants. The earth should not be wet for twenty-four hours before nor for twenty-four hours after the tonic is applied. Its results amply reward one both for the time consumed in administering and for the expense. The application may be repeated in ten days, and afterward every three weeks, if advisable.

Sheep manure, either in liquid form or used dry, is an excellent fertilizer for perennials.

Then, there is nitrate of soda, which does not stimulate root-growth, but is valuable in producing rapid increase in bloom and tends to give more brilliant coloring to the blossoms. This product should be regarded, however, as a quickening tonic, for use somewhat as nitro-glycerine is prescribed by the medical profession.

No fertilizer will produce such quick results as nitrate of soda if properly used, but, if used too freely, probably no other fertilizer can damage the plants so quickly. Nitrate of soda should be used as sparingly as one sprinkles sugar upon berries or cereal. In the rose garden, my men make a little trench a few inches from the stalk, around each rose-bush or tree, and about two inches deep, scatter in it the nitrate of soda, and cover with earth; when the whole garden has been thus treated, we turn on the water, which then gently washes the tonic to the roots of the roses. This has been done the past two years about May 10th, and again the middle of July, with excellent results.

Snapdragons which have been started in a hotbed in March, and set out in the garden in mid-May, will begin to bloom early in June, and if the soil in which they are grown is rich and some fine bone meal be dug about them when first set out, and if also they receive a dose of liquid cow manure every two weeks, they will continue to send up stalwart stalks of flowers into late fall, and until quite thick ice has formed.

I know an excellent woman gardener whose greatest specialty is the successful raising of stocks and snapdragons, and whose plants bloom continuously with strong, tall stalks and flowers of wonderful size and color. Last year, in mid-October, she shifted to a small greenhouse snapdragons and stocks that had bloomed in the garden for five months, when, the tops having been cut down somewhat, they soon began to bloom again. The middle of March, she sent me a great box of them. Allowing for a month's time to recuperate after being transplanted to the greenhouse, these two annuals bloomed continuously for nine months.

This friend is often accused of having special and secret processes for raising her snapdragons, but, although she and her gardener look very wise, they disclaim any treatment other than that described, with the addition of plenty of water.

The Poudrette can be dug about phlox and hollyhocks soon after they start to grow, and a second dose given the phlox, when the heads of their first blossoms have been cut off, will assist the plants greatly in forming their sec-

A BIT OF PINK BORDER

ond crop. But there is really nothing better than cow manure for the phlox, and, also, if used in limited quantities, for hollyhocks.

It is not generally known that the *Richardia alba*, or white calla lily, which is a native of Egypt and flourishes in the rich alluvial soil on the banks of the Nile, also growing successfully in California in irrigated fields, can be grown with excellent effect in one's garden, if started by March 1st in the hotbeds in very rich soil and given a daily soaking.

The plants may be set out when the ground is warm, in May, but the earth of the bed where they are to grow should be made rich with cow manure. The beds must always be well watered once a day, and in dry weather, twice. About half a trowelful of bone meal dug about each plant when first set out will greatly assist them.

Last summer, I planted sixty calla lilies in a large bed, set white snapdragons between them, and edged the bed with giant white fringed petunias. The effect was all that could be desired until the middle of July, when the rich soil and abundant watering (for even when in the drought water had become the most precious of fluids, this bed was kept wet) caused the snapdragons and petunias to vie with each other in such rampant growth that the calla lilies were almost crowded out of existence, so that it would seem better to plant the calla lilies in a mass by themselves.

Bon Arbor applied to petunias, heliotropes, verbenas, asters, stocks and dahlias, produces marvelous results; the blossoms are unusual in size and brilliant in color and it seems as if one could almost see the plants grow.

Last year, the seeds of the twentieth Century dahlias were sown in the hotbeds in March. They germinated quickly and grew so rapidly that they crowded against the glass, which made it necessary to transplant them to the garden quite early in May. They were set in ordinary garden soil, not very rich, and at once treated with applica-

Decorative effect of a potted plant

tions of Bon Arbor, with the result that the first blossom made its appearance May 25th, an unprecedented time for dahlias to bloom. All the other varieties of dahlias were similarly treated with Bon Arbor and between the applications watered copiously, being kept as moist as the Japanese Iris, resulting in great luxuriance of bloom with perfection of form and color. When, however, drought set in, and the sun burned daily through its course, and the southwest wind ceased not to blow, evaporating immediately the scanty supply of water given the plants, their bloom was greatly diminished, and we became convinced that, in addition to this particular fertilizer which seemed to agree with it, the dahlias need continuously an ample supply of water.

A farmer's wife, who took a first prize at the county fair for a collection of dahlias, told me that she poured all her wash-water on the ground over their roots. The potash from the soap as well as the water may be valuable for dahlias.

The verbenas responded to the tonic of Bon Arbor by remaining a sheet of color from June until late in October, and the giant ruffled petunias were indeed giants of their kind.

Heliotrope and stocks, as well as the asters, were most grateful for their meals of Bon Arbor, the heliotrope yielding clusters the largest and darkest in color we have ever raised. They seemed to be unaffected by the drought, and continued to bloom until killed by the frost.

Stocks will benefit by a small amount of bone meal given them when first set out and again at the end of two months; and if the asters, when ready to bud, receive, in addition to the Bon Arbor, a little wood-ashes, together with a very little nitrate of soda, and have, besides, rich soil and plenty of water, they will produce larger flowers and more abundantly.

All the campanula family, especially the *Campanula medium*, the Canterbury bell,

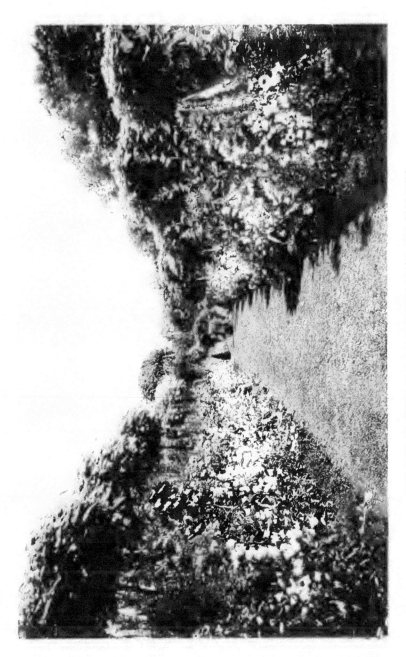

THE GARDEN WHEN THE CANTERBURY BELLS ARE BLOOMING

like a soil rich with cow manure, and if given a trowelful of bone meal about the end of April will produce wonderful plants, astonishing one in June by the amount of blossoms which each plant will bear. The foxgloves, while preferring a soil in which leafmold predominates, do finely in the borders and are also glad of some bone meal in April. This tonic is also essential for the roses, and should be given them in the spring and again in midsummer.

Sheep manure administered to the Japanese anemones, either dry, when a trowelful may be dug about the plants every month after growth begins in the spring, or applied in liquid form at three-weeks intervals, results in marvelous growth, two-year-old plants sending up many stalks of their beautiful blossoms.

If sheep manure be fed in the same manner to the salpiglossis, the effect is equally satisfactory.

Constant iteration of the need of fertilizer

becomes tiresome, but herbaceous plants and flowering shrubs are great feeders, and, as they must be closely planted to secure good effect, the soil soon becomes exhausted, and the spring feeding and entire remaking of herbaceous borders every three or four years is a necessity if one would have the finest plants.

Shortly after my first book was published, a somewhat elderly man friend whose mind is delightfully cultivated, whose sole recreation is the study of English literature, and who knows no more about gardening than about the construction of flying-machines, remarked that it was painful to make such a criticism, but it seemed to him somewhat shocking that a nice woman (the *nice* probably meaning refined) should so often refer to manures.

Now, as may be imagined, this was far more painful for me to hear than for him to say. Meeting, shortly after, a woman who was an excellent and enthusiastic gardener, whose "sensibility" even Jane Austen might have admired, I asked her honest opinion upon the subject, and was told in reply that in her experience, also, all success in gardening depended upon the preparation and fertilization of the soil, and that without manures nothing could be done; she further told me that in answer to her husband's inquiry one day, what he should give her for a birthday present, she had answered, "Two carloads of manure for the garden."

After the animal manures, decomposed vegetable matter, which the expert now refers to as humus, is the most valuable constituent of the soil. This material is within the reach of every one who has even a small place. By gathering and saving carefully all the autumn leaves, turning them several times during the year until they are decomposed, you will have them in condition to return to the soil in the form of humus or leaf-mold, and give to the plants the nitrogen so necessary to their growth.

Two years ago I attacked an herbaceous border that had not been made over for five years, only top-fertilized during that time. The border is a hundred and sixty feet long and about twelve feet wide, with an irregular edge. Many varieties of perennials grew in it whose colors had become mixed, and it was far from satisfactory. First, all the plants were lifted and the bed dug out, then twelve wagonloads of cow manure, two hundred pounds of bone meal, a quantity of leaf-mold, with a good sprinkling of both lime and wood-ashes, were put in and thoroughly incorporated with the soil; the border was then planted with choice varieties of phlox, massed in shades carefully blended of cherry, pink, and white; at intervals, groups of the taller varieties were brought toward the front, to prevent a rigid line; occasional groups of foxgloves were also planted, and the whole border was edged with sweet williams in the same colors, which are taken out when they have finished blooming and fol-

The Lily and Iris garden

lowed by asters in shades of pink. The border contains about eight hundred plants of phlox, about five hundred foxgloves, and innumerable tulips, both early and late, carefully set in sand, planted wherever there was room for a bulb. For four months this border is continuously effective in color, ranging from cherry to white.

Very fine horn shavings, dissolved in the proportion of a peck to a kerosene-oil barrel of water, and stirred well every day for three days, and then a pint of this solution poured upon the earth every two weeks, for cannas, dracænas and all foliage plants, has wonderful effect. This fertilizer is much used in Germany. Vaughn, of New York, is the only seedsman who catalogues it.

Scotch soot, applied twice a month to foliage plants, a little being dug lightly into the soil, increases the brilliancy of their color.

If one could only invent some treatment or some fertilizer that would prolong the period of bloom of the peonies, or produce a second crop of the blossoms of these most beautiful flowers, what a benefactor to gardeners that person would be! I have often thought of addressing a petition to the great Burbank upon the subject.

During the last five years the peonies in my garden have been fed about August 15th, at the same time with and similarly to 'asparagus, with cow manure and bone meal, and the wonderful increase in the size of the plants and in the number of blooms leads me to believe that the blossom-bearing buds of peonies, like those of asparagus, form in August or September for the flowers of the following year.

By this treatment, with the addition of a winter mulch of cow manure which is lightly forked into the ground as soon as frost is out in the spring, and about half a trowelful of nitrate of soda sprinkled over the crown of each plant and immediately watered in, the asparagus is made to yield abundantly from about the first of May to the middle of June, when it rests for a month. Then we again have asparagus for three weeks, and cease cutting it while still bearing freely, for fear of injuring the roots.

The number of plant diseases increases so rapidly that the harried gardener no sooner has conquered one trouble than another appears, and the spray-machine is in constant use in the fight against insect destroyers and microbe diseases. Vigilance which enables one to detect an enemy in the very beginning, and constant care, generally win the fight against everything but the terrible drought, where one is powerless. Even though the water-supply remains sufficient, the continued dryness of the atmosphere, dewless nights, constant winds, with the sun burning down upon the lawns and gardens, destroy their vitality and check their growth. In dry weather, constant stirring of the soil to the depth of a couple of inches to maintain a loose mulch, or a mulch of leaves, lawn clippings or old manure, are our greatest hope. I often feel as if all battles against plant diseases, insects and microbes might be won without serious disaster, and happiness might reign always in our gardens, if only we could have abundant rains; but to see the plants which started bravely into life in the spring begin to wither and starve from drought when midsummer luxuriance should be reached, is almost unbearable for those who love their flowers.

A new disease has very recently appeared in our gardens which I have not heard called by name. It is a blight which attacks the larkspurs, particularly the taller varieties, causes the leaves first to turn black, then to shrivel and fall off, and blights and blackens the blossom. Kelway of England, the largest grower of delphiniums, says that he has never known any disease to attack these plants in his nursery, and, until the middle of last June, my garden has been equally immune. Fearing that the trouble might prove contagious,

I took the drastic method of digging up all the plants attacked—between forty and fifty, which was a large proportion of the nearly six hundred growing in the garden—and burned them. Alas! a number of these were from eight to ten years old, and the largest, oldest and most vigorous plants in the garden, so that it was a heart-rending operation both to me and to the men. All the remaining plants were immediately sprayed with Bordeaux mixture, which spraying was repeated every month. This coming spring, when the plants first start, they will again be well sprayed and the ground over the roots also thoroughly wet with the Bordeaux, and this treatment will be given them twice afterward at intervals of three weeks, in the hope that the devastating trouble will thus be conquered. Several of the veronicas were afflicted in the same way, and were given the same prescription.

From many gardens comes a complaint of mildew affecting the climbing roses, some of the hybrid teas, and the phlox, more particularly the white and light varieties. No one knows why mildew should appear upon plants grown in full sun, when it is a disease supposed to appear only in shady places or after a considerable period of very warm, damp weather. Mildew increases with mushroom-like rapidity. An instance of this occurred in the great phlox border in my garden late last June. I had been away for two days only. All of this time the men had been employed at the other end of the place, and no one had made a daily tour, with the keen lookout for trouble that is as necessary in the flower garden as in the nursery of young children, and upon returning home late in the afternoon I made, as is customary after an absence, a careful tour of the place, when to my amazement and horror I found that several clumps, of probably fifty each, of my loveliest variety of pale pink phlox were so covered with mildew as to resemble giant plants of dusty miller. Early the next morning they were all dug up, the tops cut down to the roots, the plants then set in a row in the vegetable garden, and a mixture of equal parts of soot and flowers of sulphur powdered over them. All the other phlox in the garden, were first sprinkled and then treated with the soot and sulphur—and rather ghastly they looked.

The sick plants that had been transferred suffered from being removed in full summer, and a number of them died, but the survivors came up without a trace of mildew.

Setting rows of plants in the vegetable garden has become so constant an occurrence that my men now often ask "Where?" and say there is no more room, or that soon the vegetable garden will be nothing but a flower garden.

The Garden Club of Philadelphia, an association of enthusiastic and earnest women gardeners, each of whom is her own head gardener, have, by attention, experiment and observation, made many valuable discover-

THE PRACTICAL FLOWER GARDEN

ies upon the treatment of special plants, fertilizers and insecticides.

From them I learned of a death-dealing dose for the omnipresent rose bug which has reduced this pest in my own garden to a few survivors easily destroyed by hand.

MIXTURE FOR ROSE BUGS

3 pints of any kind of sweet milk
3 pints of kerosene
1 quart of water

Mix in something that can be shaken,—a demijohn is excellent,—shake for a few minutes, add one-half pint of the mixture to one gallon of water, stir well, then spray this diluted mixture on the rose bushes, also wet the ground thoroughly over the roots, and apply it gently with the fingers to the rose buds. It should be used every ten days from May 1 to the middle of June, and as the larvæ of the rose bug are in the ground, this treatment seems to prevent them from coming to life, and relieves us from one of our greatest trials. The same treatment may be given

140

A simple gateway

to the white Japanese iris, as the rose bugs delight also to feed upon this choice flower.

The most efficient remedy for the thrip, the small yellow-white fly, which settles upon the under side of the leaves of the rose bushes, and so devours them that soon only the skeleton of a leaf remains, is spraying with a solution of whale-oil soap; two applications a week apart will destroy them, but the odor from the whale oil is unpleasant for twenty-four hours, particularly so at the sunset hour; it is a good plan, therefore, to be absent when the whale-oil soap is used.

The rose caterpillar is hatched from the egg of a moth, rolls itself in the green leaves of the bushes, and seems to be unaffected by any poison. As this creature has a voracious appetite and devours both the young rose buds and the green leaves, he must be gotten rid of in some way. But, until now, hand-picking seems to be the only effective way.

A solution of London purple, one-half pound to fifty gallons of water, sprayed upon the aster plants when the buds begin to form, seems to be a preventive for the aster beetle, another of the garden's deadly enemies. Slug shot and lime, one pound of each, well mixed, are also efficacious weapons in the fight against this black wretch.

It would seem as if no possible success with flowers could be worth all the trouble of fertilizing and spraying and careful watching that is necessary; but, believe me, much of the interest lies in making the experiment and the effort, and if you put up a good fight you generally win out in the end and have the great satisfaction of succeeding.

The flower gardener cannot become lazy. She must not think that by merely planting zinnias, nasturtiums and poppies, she has done the whole duty of a gardener, but she must be willing to study the soil in order to find out what her plants like to eat; she must learn about insecticides in order to protect her flowers from the hungry creatures waiting to destroy them; she must find which plants live best together; she must be willing to take up her borders and make them over every three or four years; she must think ahead and plan one year for the next; she should also have patience and be willing to endeavor next year to succeed with that which has been a failure this year; she must also be a person of much courage, because there will be years when the rose bugs, the black beetle and the white grub will appear in swarms and do their worst; when the rust will destroy the hollyhocks, mildew whiten her choice plants, and drought finish almost everything else. There will come times when she will declare that she will plough up the whole garden and plant potatoes and go off and spend the summer in Europe; but, on the other hand, there will be years when her summer will be one of joy, for her peonies and iris will be magnificent, the many-shaded larkspur towering and luxuriant, the rose bugs absent in some distant state, and her song will be one of continual triumph.

Such a time of delight was mine last spring. It was in May, and a party of choice spirits gathered at the old farmhouse on a Friday, to spend Sunday. They arrived in the midst of a cold rainstorm,—one of those storms which so often comes in May, and which the farmer calls the blossom storm. Gathering about the great log fire at nightfall, we wondered how the tender growing things without could survive, and one of my friends, a man whose name is known and whose books are read wherever people care for art and literature, said to me over the tea-cups "Have you not a garden or something?" and after acknowledging something of a garden, I, in turn, inquired if he cared for gardening. He answered, " No; there is generally an angel in the pool, and there are always gravel walks, and I hate to walk upon gravel walks, and besides, I have a garden in my imagination where there are only white flowers surrounded with green setting." When I went to bed that night I leaned out of the window to see what was the

144

prospect of fair weather for the next day; the rain was coming down steadily, the wind howled up the valley, the great locusts towering over the roof tossed their arms about in distress, and fair weather seemed far distant. But in the early morning the robins were singing their May song, the sunshine was brilliant, and all without seemed to be a new created world. I could scarcely wait until the grass had dried off a little to invite my friend to come out with me to the garden. Standing at the entrance we looked down upon the hemlock hedges tipped with fresh green; upon all the evergreens clothed in their spring garments; the box edging was covered with new growth; the turf was thick and fine and, surrounded by this green setting, there were certainly two thousand blossoms of the German iris, Silver King, silvery white as its name indicates,—and my friend was able to see with his eyes the garden of his imagination. Such a moment repays one for many seasons of battle with insects and bugs, with

the rust that destroyeth in the noonday and
with the burning drought.

My own garden has been struggled with
and worked over and developed gradually
for many years, perhaps a quarter of a century (a quarter of a century seems much
longer than twenty-five years); but I sometimes wish that it had all been planned out
at the beginning by some landscape architect,
although it might then lack in natural charm.

Unless one has had great experience, a
country place should be planned by an expert.
One may choose a person whose work is satisfactory elsewhere, and who is likely to lend
an ear to the pleas of the owner; but when
once planned and planted, if a woman cares
at all about gardens and flowers, other than
American Beauty roses with three feet of
stem and moon-faced chrysanthemums, she
should maintain the position of being her own
head gardener. Her garden will thus become
an expression of her own individuality and be
quite different from those of her neighbors.

An old brick terrace

She should herself decide what she wishes to have planted, and where and how. If a garden is in charge of a professional gardener, he will generally do that which is being done by the other men of his kind in the neighborhood, so that the garden will be like any one of a dozen. By taking this personal interest in her garden the owner's health will be greatly benefited, she will maintain her activity and, above all, there will be an added interest in life. The more time and thought we spend upon our gardens and our plants, the dearer they will become, and because of this constant contact with nature, though our years may be many, we cannot grow old because of the eternal Spring that reigns in our hearts.

> "A garden is a lovesome thing, God wot,
> Rose plot, fringed pool, ferned grot;
> The veriest school of peace.
> And yet the fool contends that God is not.
> Not God in gardens when the eve is cool!
> Nay, but I have a sign;
> 'Tis very sure God walks in mine."

147

A LITTLE ABOUT TERRACES AND THEIR TREATMENT

CHAPTER VI

A LITTLE ABOUT TERRACES AND THEIR TREATMENT

THE castles and houses of landed gentry in Europe were often built, in earliest times, with terraces, which served as a viewpoint, a place to walk and take the air, and for the beginnings of gardening which were carried on in some sheltered corner of the terrace between the castle, or house, and the surrounding walls. Here the monks in the monastery first grew herbs and simples, a few flowers, and the earliest cultivated vegetables and fruits. Here, in the unsettled times of the Middle Ages, the women of the household took their recreation, and found a refuge from the eternal tapestry web or singing to the lute, and also tended the herbs with which cooling draughts and healing dressings were prepared for their lords when wounded in the fray.

The terrace, but a step or two below the house, is an open space inviting one to out-of-doors, commanding a view either across the distant country, or of smooth lawns with pond or stream beyond, or looking directly down upon the formal flower garden, and is a delightful adjunct to the modern country houses, however modest, recently built in the Northern and Middle States. The advantages of the terrace have become so convincing that the piazza, formerly of almost universal construction in the country, is being gradually dispensed with.

An objection sometimes made against the terrace is its lack of protection from sun and wind and weather. But awnings may be readily and simply put up, and if the terrace surrounds either two sides, or a portion of two sides, of the house, there will always be some place free from too strong sun or wind. For pavement, brick, red tile, marble or flat fieldstones of irregular shape are used, according to the style of the house.

Our own house, built before the War of the Revolution, which has only small porches at the entrances, has a simple terrace laid in old brick in herring-bone pattern. Circular openings surround the bases of the locust trees which grow near the house, and in these spaces the earth is covered with periwinkle— blue in April and May with its starry flowers, and green-leaved all the year. The evergreen vine, *Euonymus radicans*, is planted around the trees, and, clinging to the beautiful rough bark of the locusts, climbs far up among their branches. It is entirely hardy in the severest winters, and in March bravely sends forth tender new leaves to herald the spring. Both the lovely periwinkle and the euonymus are a delight during every month of the year.

Should the ground fall away rapidly from the house, there must, of necessity, be either a bank of turf or a retaining-wall of stone, brick or otherwise. The bank of green turf is, however, except where the house is elaborate or Italian in style, more attractive, particularly if the house is not immediately adjacent to the garden, but is surrounded only by green lawn and shrubbery. When an Italian garden is spread before a house of French or Italian architecture, the terrace must naturally be adorned with formal balustrades and whatever effects may be in keeping with house and garden of such design. Formerly, many flowers were grown close about our own old house, but for years they have been banished to a distance, except those grown in pots for terrace decoration, and only ferns, rhododendrons, small evergreens, trees and vines grow near. This may be considered severe treatment, but flowers are grown in such abundance elsewhere that the change is an improvement.

A few flowering plants, especially grown in pots for decoration of terraces or verandas, add greatly to their attraction, and are perhaps a survival of the use of the terrace in early times as a garden spot.

Those who have traveled in Spain and Italy
will remember the effective use made by
gardeners in those countries, of potted plants
upon terraces, verandas, on doorsteps, and in
courtyards, and also that only the red earthen
flower-pot, or the simple, dull green-glazed
Italian or Spanish pottery are used,—elaborate pots and jars which detract from the
beauty of the flowering plants being avoided.

A few plants well suited for terrace or
veranda where there is partial shade are: the
old-fashioned fuchsias which bloom continually; gloxinias; any of the lilies which may
be carefully lifted from the garden when about
three inches high, potted, two or more in a
pot according to size, and the pots sunk to
the brim in the ground, to be brought forward
on the terrace as they come into bloom, and
asters and salvias which may be treated in
the same way. A decoration of several pots
of white ostrich-plume asters followed by pink
ones is always admired. Schizanthus or butterfly flower, and the new yellow or pink

celosia remain beautiful for several weeks and
are especially suited for pot culture and adornment of terraces.

All those whose houses are surrounded by
terraces will find great interest in growing a
succession of plants in pots for decoration;
half a dozen pots of a kind would be sufficient unless the terrace is very large; and
even if there is no flower garden, but just a
little corner where the plants can be raised
and nursed into perfection to bring forward,
they will give an infinite amount of pleasure.

The tall-growing *Campanula pyramidalis* is
especially beautiful. Large, strong plants, one
year old in May, if potted and fed often
with liquid manure, bone meal and a tiny bit
of nitrate of soda, will be six feet high by the
the second week in August, and remain covered with either white or blue blossoms for a
month. This plant can be seen in its greatest
perfection at the Church of St. Anne de
Beaupré on the St. Lawrence River, below
Quebec, and is used there, growing in pots in

great quantities, both white and pale blue, as a decoration for the altar and chancel, and surpasses any perennial plant I have ever seen. These plants should be grown in partial shade, to secure the best success. They do not bloom until from fifteen to seventeen months after the seed has been sown in the open ground, and sometimes go over until the third summer before blooming; but no trouble is too great to grow this grand campanula successfully.

Pink and white Canterbury Bells (*Campanula medium*) which remain for several weeks in bloom, and great plants of cosmos, lifted from the garden and set in tubs, make beautiful decorations.

Where people are disinclined to raise flowering plants for the terrace, small retinisporas, in the different colorings, will be quite satisfactory when used with bay or box trees, to give height.

Bay and box trees are expensive, but long-lived if given moderate care, and the white and pink oleanders which flower continually are also well worth a place on the terrace or in the garden. These three varieties need only to be kept clean, nourished, given enough water, not allowed to freeze, and occasionally re-tubbed.

When the tubs containing bay and box trees and oleanders are brought forth from their winter quarters, they require immediate attention. They should first be watered with a strong force to cleanse them thoroughly, and then looked over for scale, which should be carefully scraped away; if the bay trees have accumulated any black mildew, it can be scrubbed off with a nail-brush, which, although a long and slow process if the trees are large, is the only one which is effective. The trees should then be sprayed with a strong solution of Ivory soap, some of the earth removed from the top of the tubs, and some soot, which is the best fertilizer for bay and box trees, dug in about the roots, and the tub then filled up with cow manure. The tubs

The formal quality of trained Ivies

may then be painted, when the trees are ready for the season's duty.

Second only to the bay tree in formal decoration is English ivy grown in tubs and trained over wire frames, pyramidal in form, which may be had from three to seven feet or more in height. The ivy covers the frame completely and compactly. Tubs of ivy can be placed to advantage at the top of a flight of steps, along the edge of a terrace, by a doorway, at the entrance to a garden, and have the merit of not being very expensive. Unless one is sure that the ivy is hardy, it should join the bay and box trees in their winter quarters.

Hardy ivy, or *Euonymus radicans*, trained to grow as a flat border about eighteen inches in width along the edge of the terrace that is upheld by a bank of turf, gives a formal finish that is satisfactory. Box edging a foot in height can also be used in this way.

The tubs containing American arborvitæ or different varieties of cedars, both of which

THE WILD GARDEN

The Terraces, Fayrewold

CHAPTER VII

THE WILD GARDEN

FOR years I have been writing of a type of garden familiar to me through long experience. Now, however, I am about to describe briefly another form of plant culture and gardening of which I have had little personal experience, but the possibilities of which I have observed for many years, during which I have watched the beginning, progress and development of a great natural or wild garden.

The term "wild garden" may be as descriptive of the garden made from native material without cultivation of the soil, and as expressive of native resources, as the terms English garden or Italian garden, where the yews of England and cypress of Italy give at once the dominant note peculiar to the country where each is situated.

Within the boundaries of every country place of any extent there will always be found the border of a woodland, a bit of marshy ground through which winds a tiny stream or a ridge of rocks, which await only the proper treatment of the possibilities they offer to become most exquisite corners upon the place.

This wild gardening presents infinite possibilities. It deals with all the native blooming plants indigenous to the locality, or that will grow there naturally under its conditions of soil and climate without cultivation, from the tiniest flowers of meadow, glade and rockledge, the innumerable growths of the bog, the ferns from the woods and borders of streams, to the towering weeds of late summer, and the many native shrubs.

The run-down and neglected farms that are scattered throughout our eastern states afford the opportunity for the practical development of this wild gardening because of their natural conditions and the

At the foot of the Terrace

infinite variety of plant life growing there naturally. Upon a few acres of land may often be found all the charm of uplands, of open fields sloping swiftly to the wooded valley, of meadows through which a stream or creek makes its way, and of rocky ledges and great boulders.

The land that once was cultivated is now overrun with many beautiful varieties of trees and shrubbery growing naturally. Here, perhaps, a group of long-neglected apple trees; there, upon a hillside, many of the native shrubs, bayberry, huckleberry, alder, sumach, pigeonwood, dogwood, shad bush, and beautiful cedars, many of them tall and symmetrical and of wonderful color, while younger seedlings are struggling to show themselves above the shrubs and tall weeds.

In the humble huckleberry bush there is constantly varying color, especially effective when it occurs in masses. The opening leaves in spring are a lovely pale yellow-green, in June the bushes are covered with tiny white flowers, in midsummer with blue berries, while in autumn the foliage turns a deep red with tints of bronze, and all through the winter the branches of the bushes are tipped with varying shades of red.

In woodlands, particularly where the big timber has been cut, will be found wonderful growths of laurel. From the foot of some great ledge of rock a little spring flows forth, sending its tiny trickle down to the bog or brook. Some of these bogs are composed of floating tussocks where grows the swamp maple, the earliest tree to attire itself in autumn coloring. Upon the low meadows are found in luxuriance the flowers of late summer and autumn,—the Joe Pye weed and other eupatoriums, starwort and goldenrod. Along the ledges of rock, where there is shade, grow luxuriantly many mosses and the winter evergreen fern; there, too, can be found the more beautiful lycopodium with its curious tufted stems, and in sunny places in the narrow crevices of the rocks the tiniest spring flowers make a home, among which is the fairy-like wind-flower.

Upon a shaded bank in the woods, where the soil is of leaf-mold and the rock-ledge gives protection, will be found the Solomon's seal, and such a spot is also the habitat of the lovely trillium, which, in several varieties—white, red and purple—dots the ground.

In more open and sunny woods there will bloom, in earliest spring, varieties of anemone, yellow dog-tooth violets, single blue violets, snakeroot, Jack-in-the-pulpit, hepatica, and the bloodroot.

Along old walls and fences are tangles of beautiful wild growth, including clematis, wild grape and Virginia creeper. The open fields and meadows are abloom with wild carrot, daisies, buttercups and wild violets. In a swampy spot where ice lies all the winter and water stands in early spring, the marigold makes a brilliant flame of yellow.

The old mill-pond, where, perhaps, only the dam and water-run, with the ruin of the mill, remain, gives a wonderful opportunity for a water-garden, where the native pond-lilies, the giant arrowhead, the water hyacinth and the pickerel weed may be planted. Many reeds and iris may fringe its edges, and swamp willows, maples and white birches may extend protecting arms over the quiet, secluded water.

At the head of such a pond, the shy, brilliant cardinal flower will be found in its home, and lovely ferns will grow in the cool moisture along the banks.

It would be impossible, in this short chapter, to enumerate a tithe of all the native growth available for such a wild garden, and those mentioned are chosen at random. A recent bulletin of the state of Connecticut, describing "the flowering plants and ferns of Connecticut, growing without cultivation," enumerates more than eight hundred species, which will afford some idea of the infinite variety of native plants available for such a garden.

Connecticut garden foreground and woodland borders

Of the flowers called wild, some are "garden escapes," the seeds of which have come from cultivated gardens where they flourished generations ago; others are "adventive," natives of foreign lands, among which are many of our common weeds which have spread in the same manner.

All of the wild plants can be made to grow without cultivation if they are given the surroundings they require. A plant which in its natural condition demands shade and moisture would not thrive on a sunny upland, nor will those flowers which need sun and a location not too damp flourish on the borders of a shaded stream.

The banks of a stream overgrown and cluttered with leaves and dead branches may be cleared away and planted with moisture-loving things—marigolds, wild violets, cardinal flower, turtle-head and the wild rose. If, here and there, rocks crop out, moss, taken up in great masses, may be brought to grow upon them.

At some convenient season, every one of these plants may be taken up with care, and, if properly planted in the situation each demands, they will go on growing serenely. These native plants may even be lifted, transported from almost any distance not too great, and so replanted that, the following day, there will be no suspicion that they have not always lived there on the banks of the little stream, or wherever they may have been set.

A peaty bog will usually be filled with wild roses, azaleas and sweet pepper. Sometimes these bushes cling to the rocks in a network of fibrous roots, making a foot-hold in the leaf-mold which gives them life. They may be stripped from the rocks intact and taken away to plant elsewhere. In dry times, when the swamps are accessible, the bushes that grow in the rich, wet soil can be taken up with a solid ball of earth around the roots and replanted with certainty of living.

Lilium Canadense and *L. Philadelphicum*

Brook side descending lane

may be staked when blooming, and taken up in the autumn, to plant where wanted.

Trees growing in wet places, which are accessible only in dry times, may easily be transplanted. A circle some three feet from the trunk of the tree should first be dug around it, then from the circle a ditch should be opened, to lead away the water, and the whole left for a year to dry out. When the tree becomes accustomed to the drier soil, it may be transplanted wherever desired.

I have seen tulip trees twenty feet high, thus treated, transplanted successfully from swamp to open ridge. For use in transplanting, a stout carrier may be made of hickory poles with cross slats nailed closely together, light but strong, which can be taken into fields inaccessible to wagon, and will serve to carry out the plants and shrubs.

The farmer's "stone boat" performs the same service for larger things, such as small trees, bayberries, billberries, great bushes of laurel, etc.

THE PRACTICAL FLOWER GARDEN

If a field quite "run out," as the farmer expresses it, is to be tilled, some of the sod, which is often full of lovely wild flowers, may be taken up and brought to the wild garden. Thus transplanted, the blossom will not even droop for a day.

If fences are to be straightened and rebuilt, the beautiful bushes and vines which have adorned their dilapidation may also be transplanted into the wild garden.

The bogs, wet meadows and swamps, whether your own or your neighbor's, are your nurseries, and permission for such transplanting will seldom be refused. But such constant reclamation is now being carried on all over the country that, if you see any plant or shrub you want growing in swamp or bog, you should lose no time in securing it for your natural garden; for bog and swamp may soon be drained and reclaimed and used for onion meadow or corn field, when its day as a nursery for wild flowers will be gone.

In the practice of wild gardening, the win-

174

ter becomes no less interesting than the summer.

Winter is the best time, not only to get at, but to transplant, many shrubs. They may be dug about during a thaw when the ground is soft, and allowed to stand until the ball of earth about the roots is frozen again, when they can be taken up and planted without even knowing it themselves.

In late fall, when people are returning to town from their country-places, leaving the tender roses and other plants wrapped in straw, the fountain stilled and housed for the winter, loneliness and desolation hold sway in the cultivated garden, but the natural garden is still full of lovely things. Evergreen fern, ground pine and wintergreen, with scarlet berries, carpet the ground; the bayberry bush with its dull silver berries, the red-stemmed dogwood, the dark sumach, the red hips of the wild rose, the orange berries of the bittersweet, the glossy-leaved laurel and the waving plumes of goldenrod

Elm gate vista

tones we so often see in paintings, which give a singular charm known only to those who seek the country in winter.

The winter is the best time for planting, and transplanting also, for the reason that, then, every detail of the landscape is open to view and more clearly defined. A tree which in the summer you might decide to remove or cut down will often be allowed to remain if you wait until winter to see its trunk and branches against the sky, and their effect in the winter landscape.

Do not think this wild gardening exists merely in imagination. I have a friend who has planned and developed just such a garden and has produced one of the most beautiful pieces of natural planting that can be found anywhere. He calls it the "Connecticut Garden." This name was chosen, half in jest, half in earnest, to prove the possibility of making a garden of the natural plants and shrubbery which grow wild in Connecticut, and which, under favorable conditions, may be grouped

177

in effective planting and there grown without cultivation. The object of the garden was to grow effectively, in their natural conditions, those plants which would live without cultivation or specially prepared soil. It is a garden where no seeds are sown, no fertilizer used, and where the ground is not tilled. Even wild roses, when transplanted from one part of the place to another, such as the Blanda and others, of which there are forty-three varieties native in Connecticut, receive no fertilizer. In situations where they are much in evidence, the ground over the roots is covered with sods of moss brought from the woods. In this wild garden, roses have thriven for years, though receiving no care.

Some might call it a garden of weeds, but if the Joe Pye is a weed, so also are the wild violet, the trillium, the bloodroot and the hepatica. Those shrubs and flowers which are needed to produce an effect in mass are planted as closely together as possible, the branches even touching, while, in some other situations, only single specimens of great size are used.

In this Connecticut garden, the rock-ledges and boulders are treated as a part of the garden as much as the trees or flowers themselves, and are objects of beauty. At the foot of the boulders grow, in places, prostrate junipers, native columbines and creeping phlox. In crevices of the rock-ledge are many ferns, columbines and velvety mosses, and along the tops of the ledges grow bayberry and huckleberry bushes. If a ledge has been obscured by a tangle of briar, underbrush and fallen limbs of trees, and the crevices of the rock are full of leaves and debris, all are cleared and brushed away, leaving only the clinging evergreen fern and many varieties of moss. In some niches, leaf-mold is placed, in which tiny flowers of exquisite beauty soon appear.

These ledges of rock may be called not a rock garden, but rather a garden of rocks. Different conditions of the atmosphere—mist, sunshine and gray autumn—produce wonderful effects in their curious seams of color, and at times it is hard to say whether the rocks or the plants growing around and about them are most beautiful.

Descending the swift slope of fields stretching from the old farmhouse, and crossing a natural ravine, we pass a small pond where wild geese have found conditions so favorable that no temptations lead them away, cross a noisy brook that tumbles and sings on its way between the great boulders that line its sides, and finally come to the simple gate of white palings that opens between two graceful elms into the Connecticut garden.

Here we find a little open green, along a stone wall, extending on one side of which masses of laurel grow and prosper in full sunshine. Descending a green aisle where in spring the sod is gay with tiniest flowers of white, yellow, lavender, blue, one side of which is bordered with a tall growth of huckleberry bushes backed by hundreds of

Wild geese pool by garden approach

wild flowering shrubs, and the other by wild roses, bayberry and wild azalea, we come to a ledge of rock where stands a giant laurel. This ledge, with its steep out-cropping, and masses of boulder and shelf of rock, is bright with color from early spring. Here, in May, white creeping phlox breaks in a foam against the rock, and Columbine, dwarf rose and low-flowering shrubs of every kind grow in profusion. Down another aisle, we come to a great tulip tree, the most wonderful specimen of its kind I have ever seen.

Crossing a stream and following a narrow lane, where a little orchard of wild apple trees grows on one side and a thicket of dogwood and alder on the other, we come to the meadows composed of many acres of wild-growing native flowers.

Across these meadows, wide paths are kept open by the mowing-machine, which serve to make possible closer view and enjoyment of the many flowers which grow here. These meadows have been drained by a wide, shallow ditch, as well as by a stream which flows gently through them. Upon the rising edges of the meadow along the woodland are masses of tall asters, heleniums and elderberry; and in the meadow bloom marigold, many iris, patches of the rare fringed blue gentian, turtle head, pink, white and crimson mallow, iron weed, vervain, thoroughwort, and all the lovely growths natural to damp places, with their successively changing colors, of white, red, yellow, orange and russet. As month follows month, each species of plant rises higher and higher, each successive growth hiding the earlier one, until at last, in autumn, the great plumes of goldenrod, the many-hued starworts and the towering heleniums and helianthus reign supreme.

Looking down upon the meadows are rounded knolls covered with sparse grass, which is thickly interspersed with flowers, such as St. John's-wort, everlasting, mulleins, beautiful thistles and black-eyed susans.

Massed bed August and autumn perennials

After the flowers have seeded themselves, in the autumn, the knolls are closely cut, to bring out their contours and give emphasis to the flowery meadows below them, which latter are mown by hand with scythe or sickle only when the earliest signs of coming spring appear, raked with heavy wooden rakes and the dead material removed, when, almost immediately, the floral procession that lasts until late autumn begins to appear.

On other uprises of land above the meadows, wild apple trees are made to contribute great effect. Some twisted and stunted specimens, which in their struggle for life seldom blossom or bear fruit, have been cut away at the top until they remind us of some curious and ancient Japanese trees.

The ordinary wild apple trees, often covered thickly with red and yellow fruit which hangs upon the branches until winter, give charming detail. They overhang pathways, and are more beautiful than anything that could be planted in their places. These apples, too, are of value as food for the wild inhabitants of the garden. On a winter's day, the partridge comes for the apple seeds, and when startled into flight, makes a dash of gray into the shelter of the woods.

The wild garden is also a home for the birds; the red-winged blackbird makes his nest among the bulrushes and cat-tails; the chewink is busy in the leaves under the shrubs; the thrush finds here his favorite haunts, and also the yellow hammer, the bluejay, and all the birds of wood and thicket.

After the leaves have fallen in autumn, the nests which have been skilfully hidden among the verdure are then seen for the first time, and we become aware how very many of the shy and elusive birds have made this garden their home.

Passing along the wide pathway, through the meadow of flowers and through a thicket of willows, we come to the "shadow pond," quite concealed from view by the shrubbery

and the contour of the ground until we reach
its very edge. Here we find a water-garden
dug from the bog, with winding, irregular
banks upon which grow wild roses, tall lilies,
alder, azaleas, the sweet pepper, and in the
wet, low edges flags and grasses, and all the
water-loving plants, while pink, white and
yellow pond-lilies float upon the surface of
the water. On one side, this pond is bordered
by a great woodland which in the spring is
pink with wild azalea; across the pond, one
looks into a little glade of singular charm and
seclusion, framed in by high ledge upon ledge,
where great cedars grow naturally, and where,
in the foreground, the dominant feature is an
ancient swamp ash of wonderful symmetry
and size.

From this little glade we come to a green
meadow which has been reclaimed from a
thicket and bog, through which, along a
plantation of hornbeam, a slender stream
flows until it loses itself in the bog which
feeds the water-garden.

185

Through this Connecticut garden many paths lead, which are often carpeted with sods taken from some lean pasture or meadow, carrying with them small mosses and tiny flowers. Along one path a little orchard has been planted of the wild apple trees found on the farm, set in line with the path. Other paths lead through thickets of dogwood and alders.

By another path, we come to a corner of the garden given over to lilies, which grow in a bed by themselves,—the *Hemerocallis fulva*, or old familiar tawny day lily, the lemon day lily, the blackberry lily (all of which are garden escapes); then there are also *L. Philadelphicum*, or red wood lily, *L. superbum*, or Turk's cap lily, and the *L. Canadense*, or wild yellow lily, all of which together make a veritable garden of lilies.

Walking through the densest woods by old wood roads and narrow footpaths winding between the trees, and often following a stream, we see the frail Indian pipe that

Overlooking the "Marigold Meadow"

shrinks from the sunlight; pushing away dead leaves, we find plantations of the lovely trailing arbutus, which is fast becoming extinct as a wild flower, because of the reckless manner in which it is gathered, whole plants being too often torn up by the roots. In these woods, too, lives the maidenhair fern, loved by all who know it; and in brighter spots, growing about the foot of some great rock, is the bluebell, *Campanula rotundifolia*, which grows alike in sunshine and in shadow, in rich, mouldy soil or barren sandy hilltop.

A most beautiful path takes us through a gap in the tallest ledge of rocks, down a hillside where many cedars grow along the path, with just enough of intention to emphasize the alignment. Here, in blustering weather, no winds can penetrate, and in summer heats cool quiet dwells. In this fragrant, dense seclusion, one would fain sit and read or dream for hours. At the curve of this path we see the Gray Glen, with the tall gray trunks of swamp ash, elm, oak, tulip and whitewood growing in the Glen, through which a stream finds its way, amidst a maze of rock and boulder, down into the main river.

At all times,—in early spring, in times of freshet when the streams tumble and foam along their course, in the drought and heat of midsummer, the murmurs of the brooks and the sound of falling water as it comes down through two beautiful little glens and falls over artfully constructed dams quite hidden from view,—there is the enchantment which running water alone can give to landscape or garden. And among the greatest charms of this Connecticut garden are the river that flows along its outer boundaries, the streams, brooks and swamps running through it, and its wonderful water-supply, abundant in all seasons.

In spring, all the woods are carpeted with dog-tooth violets, anemones, and blue violets, and one cannot tread without crushing some delicate plant, while snakeroot, sweet

The Cedar Path to Gray Glen

fern, oxalis, hepaticas and the many other flowers make a garden of the woods.

Beyond, and a mile and more from the Connecticut garden, and separated from it by glades and sloping fields, upon a far end of the estate, there is a wonderful hemlock glen, where a foaming stream tumbles over its rocky bed, which lies at the bottom of a deep ravine worn out by centuries of rushing waters. This glen is bordered on both sides and banks by ancient hemlocks, through whose great branches the sunshine comes but gently; here footsteps make no sound on the needle-sown ground, gray rocks, bedded in ferns, and carpeted with many varieties of moss, invite one to sit upon their soft cushions and listen to the changing music of the stream below, while wood pigeons, flying from tree to tree, utter their soft notes, and delicious scents of sweet fern and resinous hemlock fill the air. The stream, in places dashing over water-worn boulders, sends its white spray high in air, and again hurries down many rapids, and comes to rest in clear brown pools where the sunlight sends its golden glints, and shy trout can be seen if one creeps softly to the water's edge.

With just a bite of luncheon, a book, perhaps a dog as companion, one can spend a long, delicious day in this wonderful hemlock glen, and, in late afternoon, in the level light of the sunset hour, the walk across the quiet fields to the low, gray farmhouse is not the least of the day's delights.

Standing before this quaint century-old house, a never-to-be-forgotten landscape stretches before us. To the eastward we look down on a gently sloping field of broad expanse, on the great twin elms which keep watch at the gate of the Connecticut garden, and see in the distance the rock-ledges and boulders, the flowery meadow, the dark cedars, and the general contours of the natural garden. Towards the south, we look out over tracts of woodland, much of it first growth, over orchards of twisted apple trees and smooth, green fields where sheep gather under the protecting shade of great oaks, across a wide extent of country to the distant, shimmering sea, many miles away, now blue, now gray where the sunlit sails are clearly seen.

This Connecticut garden is a unique expression of wild, or natural, gardening, which has both value and interest, and is well worth while. It is of importance, also, as an example of a development of possibilities that may be within the reach of many who, so far, have not availed themselves of opportunities lying close at hand. Here are gathered and planted, with a particular regard for appropriateness of situation and proximity, nearly all of the native plants, ferns and shrubs of Connecticut, and the locality itself is so favored that most of the wild flowers whose habitat is anywhere in the country between southern Maine and New Jersey are to be found there, the orchids of the more northern region alone being wanting.

191

The maker of the Connecticut garden has not learned his art from books, but rather from a great love of nature and a close and constant observation of her thousand phases. And he has created, through the use and development of native material only, a garden which is truly wonderful.

The brook in springtime

SHRUBS, VINES, PLANTS, AND BULBS
WHICH I HAVE GROWN
SUCCESSFULLY

SHRUBS, VINES, PLANTS AND BULBS
WHICH I HAVE GROWN
SUCCESSFULLY

HARDY SHRUBS

AZALEA MOLLIS. 2 to 3 feet. Plant only in spring. Never prune. Should have northern exposure. Must be heavily mulched and kept moist in summer. Blooms in May and early June. The most effective low-growing shrub. When blooming, it is one mass of delicate blossoms of many colors—pink, purple, crimson, lavender, red, orange, yellow and white.

Azalea mollis

195

The pink variety from the woods is, of course, hardy. The *Azalea mollis*, though very beautiful, is, however, not particularly hardy.

BERBERIS THUNBERGII (Japanese Barberry). 6 feet. Plant in early spring. Has scarlet berries in the fall that remain through most of the winter. It is very hardy and healthy, and is suitable for low hedges.

CALYCANTHUS FLORIDUS (Sweet Shrub; Strawberry Shrub). 6 to 12 feet. Plant in the spring, or in the fall not later than October 15th. Blooms in early June. With its fragrant, little, pineapple-shaped, maroon-colored flowers, it is a familiar sight in old-fashioned gardens.

CLETHRA ALNIFOLIA (White Alder; Sweet Pepper Bush). 6 to 8 feet. Plant in the spring. Blooms in July and August. The spikes of delicate, feathery white flowers have a very sweet perfume.

CORNUS FLORIDA and C. RUBRA (White- and Red-flowering Dogwood). 8 to 15 feet. Transplant from woods, or plant in the fall by October 15th, as it starts very early in the spring. Blooms in May. The large, flat, irregular flowers — either white or a purplish red — often cover the tree with a mass of color.

CRATÆGUS (Hawthorn). 10 feet. Plant in

Deutzia crenata. See page 198

197

the early spring or fall. Blooms in May and
June. It has very fragrant, delicate little
pink-and-white blossoms, both double and
single, which are followed by small red ber-

Deutzia crenata

ries. The haw-
thorn is familiar
to all readers of
English litera-
ture. In fact, it
is perhaps the
b e s t - k n o w n
English shrub.

CYTISUS LA-
BURNUM (Golden
Rain). 8 to 12
feet. Plant in the
autumn before
October 15th.

Blooms in early summer. This dwarf tree, or
large shrub, has long, drooping racemes of
bright yellow flowers.

DEUTZIA CANDIDISSIMA and D. CRENATA).
8 to 10 feet. Plant in spring or fall. Blooms

198

the end of June and July. A very beautiful and profusely blooming shrub. The small blossoms are either single or double, and come in white, pink and white tinged with pink.

FORSYTHIA FORTUNEI and F. SUSPENSA (Golden Bell). 6 to 10 feet. Plant in the fall. Blooms in April and early May. The first shrub to bloom in the spring. Its tall, straight (or, in the Suspensa, drooping)

Hibiscus

branches, covered with bright yellow bells, are a delight to the eye.

HIBISCUS SYRIACUS, ALBA PLENA, GRAND-IFLORA, SUPERBA, JEANNE D'ARC. (Althea; Rose of Sharon.) 6 to 8 feet. Plant early in

199

the spring. Blooms in July and August, when few other shrubs are in blossom. A beautiful shrub, growing very tall and straight, and particularly good for high hedges. The leaves are handsome, and the single and

Japanese Maple. See page 201

double cup-shaped flowers are purple, magenta, pink and white. The white and pale pink are lovely.

HYDRANGEA PANICULATA GRANDIFLORA. 6 feet. Plant in the spring. Blooms the end of July and August. Perhaps the best-known of all summer shrubs. The blossoms, in dense, pyramidal panicles, often a foot long, are at the end of every branch. At first white, and later changing to a russet-pink, they last for weeks. A particularly satisfactory shrub, for it blooms at a time when there is no other blossoming shrub.

JAPANESE MAPLE. 2 to 6 feet. Plant in the spring. These shrubs have no blossoms, but the brilliant tones—either red, yellow or purple—of the delicate foliage lend a most attractive note of color to shrubberies.

LIGUSTRUM OVALIFOLIUM (California Privet). 2 to 8 feet. Plant in the spring. More frequently used for hedges than any other plant; also very good as a screen. When planted in hedges it should be set out 8 to 12 inches apart. Must be pruned twice a year,— in June and August,—otherwise the plants will be " leggy," and the hedge not thick and fine.

LIGUSTRUM VULGARE (Common Privet). 2 to 8 feet. Plant in the spring. Much more hardy than the California privet and equally

good for hedges and screens. Should be set
out and pruned in the same way.

Magnolia conspicua. See page 203

MAGNOLIA CONSPICUA, M. SOULANGEANA and M. STELLA. 4 to 8 feet. Plant in early spring. Never prune. Blooms in April or May, according to the variety. A tree-like shrub, with large, smooth, shiny leaves and cup-like flowers that are white, pink and a purplish pink. They are a great source of pleasure, for they bloom at a time when there is little else. Some

Magnolia Soulangeana

old specimens are very large, and, of course, in warm climates they attain the size of trees.

PHILADELPHUS GRANDIFLORUS (Mock Orange). 6 to 10 feet. Plant in early spring or fall. Blooms in early June. A very popular and hardy shrub, covered, in blooming time, with masses of white flowers, shaped like the wild rose, and of a powerful and spicy fragrance. Very good as a screen.

PRUNUS PISSARDI (Purple-leaved Plum). 8 to 10 feet. Plant in spring or fall. A most effective shrub, with reddish purple leaves and stems that deepen in color as the season advances.

PRUNUS JAPONICA ALBA and RUBRA (Flowering Almond). Plant in early spring or fall. Blooms in May and June. A very effective shrub. The beautiful flowers are single and double, white and red.

Magnolia stella. See page 203

PYRUS JAPONICA (Japanese Quince; Burning Bush). Plant in spring or fall. Blooms in May. A very handsome shrub when it is in full bloom, for it is then one mass of brilliant red flowers.

ROSA RUGOSA (Ramanas Rose). 2 to 6 feet. Plant in early spring or fall. Blooms almost all summer. A very healthy shrub of the rose family. The large blossoms are single and double, and pink, white and crimson. Later in the year they are followed by red seed-pods. It is often used for hedges.

RHUS COTINUS (Purple Fringe, or Smoke Tree). 8 to 15 feet. Plant in the spring. Blooms in July. A tree-like shrub. When it is in bloom, the great featheriness and peculiar pinkish gray of the blossoms make the bush look as if it were enveloped in a cloud of smoke or morning mist.

SPIRÆA ANTHONY WATERER, PRUNIFOLIA, BRIDAL WREATH, THUNBERGII and VAN HOUTTEI. 4 to 8 feet. Plant in early spring or fall. Blooms the end of May and early in

June. A very beautiful shrub. In blooming time it is one mass of flowers that are white, pink, and, in some varieties, crimson. The *Spiræa Van Houttei* is perhaps the most attractive member of the family.

SYMPHORICARPOS RACEMOSUS (Snowberry). 4 to 6 feet. Plant in early spring. Blooms in August. The little pink flowers and the white wax-like berries grow side by side upon the branch. The berries remain until quite into the winter.

SYRINGA JOSIKÆA, MADAME LEMOINE, MADAME CASIMIR-PERIER, PERSICA ALBA and MARIE LEGRAYE (Lilac). 3 to 10 feet. Plant in spring or fall—before October 15th. Blooms in May and June. The long, fragrant panicles of bloom are white, pink and purple, single and double, and are familiar to all. No shrub is more satisfactory, both in blooming time and at other seasons, for the branches are heavily covered with handsome, healthy, smooth green leaves. They are, however, in some localities, subject to mildew. In these modern days of flower-culture, the lilacs have been so perfected and the

Syringa, Marie Legraye

207

varieties of Japanese, Persian, and French syringas are so numerous and varied that the catalogue of one firm alone has over fifty varieties. An at-

Lilac

tractive spring garden could be made with this shrub only, in all its many colors, shapes and families. As there are both early- and late-blooming varieties, this spring garden would be a beautiful changing color picture for fully five weeks.

VIBURNUM PLICATUM (Japanese Snowball). 6 to 10 feet. Plant in early spring or fall. Blooms the end of May and June. The foliage is healthy and dark, and the flowers grow in large balls. The sharp contrast between white flowers and very dark leaves, and the unusual manner in which the blossoms grow, make this a very effective and decorative shrub.

WEIGELA CANDIDA, EVA RATHKE and ROSEA. 6 to 10 feet. Plant in the spring. Blooms in June and July. A favorite shrub with good foliage and many trumpet-shaped flowers which are white and various shades of pink.

EVERGREEN SHRUBS

STANDARD SHRUBS

BUXUS (Dwarf, Bush, Globe-shaped, Pyramidal and Standard Box). 6 inches to 6 feet. Plant in spring. A favorite evergreen shrub with small, smooth, glossy leaves, but, in localities where the winters are severe, it is not hardy, and all box, except the dwarf varieties, must be kept in a cellar, or greenhouse, in winter. The dwarf variety will survive the severe climate only if heavily covered with straw, leaves, and even boards, which must not be removed too early in the spring, for the thawing and freezing of the first warm days will burn and hurt box even more than the cold of winter.

The dwarf box for edging flower-beds should be planted three inches apart and trimmed in June and August. The larger box plants, such as the pyramidal and standard varieties, are better grown in tubs, for they can be thus more easily moved, as it is not well for them to be too often transplanted.

LAURUS NOBILIS (Pyramidal, Tree-shaped or Standard Bay Trees). Not hardy. Must be kept indoors in winter; but in either green or white wooden tubs, or in white or red terra-cotta pots, the bay tree is invaluable as a garden or terrace decoration.

HARDY EVERGREEN SHRUBS

KALMIA LATIFOLIA (Mountain Laurel). 2 to 10 feet. Plant or transplant from the woods early in the spring or in the fall. Never prune. Does better in partial shade. Should

be well mulched and kept watered in summer.
Blooms early in June. This is a beautiful

Kalmia latifolia

211

shrub, with unusual cup-shaped blossoms that grow at the ends of the branches, and are either white or a delicate pink. The leaves are smooth, narrow and glossy. There is no more beautiful sight than the woods when the laurel is in blossom, with flowers in masses among the dark tree-trunks. Tradition has it that the foliage is poisonous to sheep, hence the country name," sheep laurel."

MAHONIA (Ashberry). Plant in the spring or fall. Blooms in May. A hardy shrub with leaves like the English holly and turning crimson in the winter; pretty yellow flowers.

RHODODENDRON MAXIMUM. 2 to 8 feet. Plant, or transplant from woods, in spring, or, in fact, almost any time before August. Never prune. Blooms in June and July according to the variety. Should be kept in partial shade. Must be heavily mulched and in summer should be always moist. The *Rhododendron maximum,* indigenous to our woods, has a pink flower that grows in clusters on the ends of the branches. It is one of those plants where the bud forms one year and the blossoms the next. Other varieties are purple, pink, mauve and white, but, unlike the Maximum, they will not thrive in very cold localities.

Rhododendron maximum

EVERGREENS

Evergreens can be set out at almost any time, from early spring until September, provided the roots are never allowed to dry until the shrub is well started. It is wiser, however, to plant or transplant from the

213

woods in early spring before the young
shoots have started, or in August after the
shrub has finished growing. All evergreens
are improved by shearing, which makes the
foliage more dense and handsome. When
grown in hedges they cannot have too
much shearing; it makes the hedge thick and
prevents it from being "leggy"; nothing
can be more unattractive than a hedge
where the branches begin a foot above the
ground.

ABIES (Spruce, or Fir). 3 feet upward.

A. ALBA (White Spruce). Of thick pyramidal growth with silvery foliage; very hardy.

A. BALSAMEA (Balsam Fir). Our familiar
Christmas tree; very hardy.

A. CANADENSIS (Hemlock Spruce). A hardy
native tree, splendid for hedges, but it is
naturally of open growth and must be
heavily sheared.

A. EXCELSA (Norway Spruce). A beautiful hardy tree, perfect in shape, with dense,
dark green foliage.

A. EXCELSA AUREA. A golden-leaved variety of Norway Spruce.

A. NORDMANNIANA. The foliage is a silver-gray above, and a duller, darker color below. A fine, hardy tree.

A. PUNGENS GLAUCA (Colorado Blue Spruce). One of the most beautiful of the evergreens. It has foliage of a decided blue tone, grows very densely and in good form, and is entirely hardy.

A. PUNGENS GLAUCA KOSTERI. A more perfected type of the Colorado Blue Spruce.

JUNIPERUS (Juniper). 3 feet upwards.

J. COMMUNIS HIBERNICA (Irish Juniper). A beautiful tree growing tall and slim and straight, like a Lombardy poplar. It is, however, rather delicate and will not live much further north than central New Jersey.

J. VIRGINIANA (Red Cedar). Indigenous to our woods and very hardy. Grows tall and straight and very compact; is a most ornamental tree and can be used to lend height and character to the garden, in the same way the Italian and Spanish gardeners use their cypress trees.

PINUS (Pine). 3 feet upward.

P. STROBUS (White Pine). One of our native pines and very hardy. It has light green foliage and will live in a poor soil.

P. SYLVESTRIS (Scotch Pine). Another very hardy, healthy, straight-growing pine that will be found most satisfactory.

RETINISPORA (Japan Cypress). 2 feet upward.

R. FILIFERA (Thread-branched). A hardy, drooping variety with large, pointed leaves. Very good to plant with straight-growing evergreens, as the sharp contrast is attractive.

R. PLUMOSA. A mass of dark green, feathery branches; much improved by shearing. Only fairly hardy.

R. PLUMOSA AUREA. A variety in which the young shoots and terminal branches are quite yellow. Not hardy north of New Jersey, but most effective among the darker evergreens. Needs much shearing to make it thick and bushy.

R. SQUARROSA VEITCHII. A low-growing, bushy variety with feathery, silvery, blue-green foliage. Hardy only south of New York except in very protected situations. In other places it must be covered in winter. It requires much shearing.

SCIADOPITYS (Umbrella Pine). 3 feet upward. A Japanese evergreen that is particularly beautiful. The foliage is in the shape of rather long, broad needles growing around a center point—a light, yellowish green above, and quite white underneath. It stands out in sharp contrast to other evergreens, and should always be planted where it can survive the winters, for it will not live much further north than New Jersey.

THUYA (Arborvitæ). 3 feet upward. All the varieties of this evergreen are hardy. Most satisfactory and best-known are:

T. ELEGANTISSIMA AUREA. The young shoots are quite yellow in summer, and in winter turn to bronze.

T. OCCIDENTALIS (American Arborvitæ). The well-known variety, excellent for hedges. Needs plenty of shearing to keep it thick.

T. SIBIRICA. A low-growing variety, with bluish green foliage; particularly hardy.

HARDY PERENNIALS

Almost all perennials can be easily grown from seed, which may be sown in the spring, or in August, in rows in the seed-bed. After careful weeding and watering, the plants will be large enough by October 1st to transplant either into rows or into the borders where they are to bloom the following year. Plants can be bought from nurserymen, and old plants of such varieties as rudbeckia, phlox, peony, larkspur, etc., may be divided.

ACHILLEA, THE PEARL (Milfoil, or Yarrow). 12 inches. Plant in the spring, or in the fall before October 15th. Blooms in June and July. Is both yellow and white, but it is far more attractive and satisfactory as a white flower.

ACONITUM NAPELLUS (Monkshood). 3 to 4 feet. Plant in October or early spring. Blooms from the end of July until frost. One of the most beautiful blue flowers, that is not usually appreciated as it should be. The individual flowers, like many little caps, make a most effective note of color in the border. It thrives better in partial shade and should be planted where it does not get the full, strong sun. The handsome leaves are sometimes affected with a black microbian disease, and, to avoid this, the plants must be sprayed in April, May and June with Bordeaux mixture.

ANCHUSA ITALICA, DROPMORE VARIETY (Sea Bugloss). 3 to 8 feet. Plant in the early spring, or in the fall before October 15th. Blooms from about June 1st for six weeks. A very healthy plant with long spikes

219

of deep blue flowers, which are very ornamental.

AGROSTEMMA CORONARIA (Mullein Pink) and A. FLOS JOVIS (Flower of Jove). (Rose Campion). 3 feet. Plant in the spring, or in the fall before October 15th. Blooms in June

Anemone

and July. This plant has silvery foliage and pink-like flowers in deep rose and crimson; very useful in the pink border.

ANEMONE JAPONICA, WHIRLWIND and ALBA (Japanese Windflower). 2 to 3 feet. Plant in the spring that it may be well established by winter. Blooms in August and September. There are red and pink varieties, but as a white flower it is one of the garden queens; and who does not always prefer a white flower? It will do well in partial shade, and is quite hardy, but needs some slight covering in winter. Can be used satisfactorily both in borders and in beds by itself.

AQUILEGIA (Columbine). 2 to 3 feet. Plant early in the spring, or after September 15th. Blooms the end of May and June. An important, beautiful perennial. The long-spurred flowers are of many beautiful colors and always a great source of delight to the flower lover. Planted in partial shade, in front of azaleas, laurel, rhododendron or ferns, it is particularly delightful.

ASTER, HARDY (Michælmas Daisy, or Starwort). 1 to 4 feet. Plant in the spring. Blooms from the middle of August until frost. Our common roadside aster; in many colors, from white through the pink, lavender and purple shades. Very effective and beautiful.

Is best in shrubberies or in the wild garden. There are many varieties—one seedsman lists one hundred and twenty-nine. A border of

hardy asters is always a beautiful addition to the garden.

BAMBOO, HARDY. 14 to 20 feet. Plant in the spring or fall. These tall grasses need a rich soil and plenty of water. They should also be heavily

Starwort

mulched, both in summer and winter, and should be planted in a sheltered position. Are particularly good against a background of native trees and along the banks of a pond or stream.

BAPTISIA AUSTRALIS and B. TINCTORIA

(False Indigo). 2 feet. Plant in the early
spring, or in the fall before October 15th.
Blooms in June and July. A healthy plant
with spikes of flowers which are dark blue
in the Australis, and yellow in the Tinctoria.
Very useful in a blue border or in the wild
garden.

BELLIS PERENNIS (English Daisy). 2 to
6 inches. Can be raised, like all perennials,
from seed sown either in the spring or in
July and August. Later, it should be transplanted to where it is to bloom. Should be
covered in winter. Blooms in May and June.
This little, ball-shaped, white-and-pink flower
is familiar to all. Generally used as an edging
for beds and borders.

BOCCONIA CORDATA (Plume Poppy). 5 to
8 feet. Plant in the spring, or in the fall
before October 15th. Blooms in July or
August. A large, decorative plant, with
handsome leaves and long spikes of small,
feathery white flowers that are succeeded
by bronze-green seed-pods. Very attractive

in shrubberies or in wild borders. It
increases rapidly.

Bocconia

SHRUBS, VINES, PLANTS AND BULBS

BOLTONIA GLASTIFOLIA and B. LATISQUAMA (False Chamomile). 4 to 6 feet. Plant in the spring, or in the fall before October 15th. Blooms in August and September. A very useful and beautiful perennial. When in bloom, it is one mass of white or pink daisy-like flowers.

CAMPANULA MEDIUM (Canterbury Bells). 3 feet. Plant in the spring, or, if the plants are already where they are to bloom, dig in around each a little manure or bone meal, in April. They should be staked. Canterbury Bells are easily raised from seed, but the seedlings should be transplanted by September 20th into the beds where they are to bloom, in order that they may be well rooted before the winter. Blooms in June and July for over a month. The most satisfactory of the Campanula family. Beautiful in borders in front of early pink phlox that should bloom at the same time, and back of the Sweet William, or Newport Pink

C. MEDIUM CALYCANTHEMA (Cup and Saucer; Canterbury Bells). 2 to 3 feet. Another form of the same flower, well described by its name.

C. PYRAMIDALIS (Chimney Bellflower). 4 to 6 feet. Plant in the spring. Blooms in July and August. The tall spikes of bloom of white or blue are quite remarkable, but, because when grown in the garden the stalks bloom irregularly—some flowers here, some there—it is not universally admired. When grown and forced in greenhouses, or in shade, the whole stalk blooms at once and is very beautiful.

CHRYSANTHEMUM, HARDY POMPON. 2 to 3 feet. Plant in the spring. Only the Pompon varieties are really hardy. They need a rich soil, and a sunny, sheltered place where they can be protected from early frosts. Bloom often into November, as only a very severe frost affects them. No buds should be allowed to form until September, and until then all shoots should be pinched back. The hardy chrysanthemums give a profusion of small, ragged blossoms, growing in clusters, and come in all the best colors—white, rose, violet-crimson, yellow, orange and brown. Old plants should be divided to about four shoots each and transplanted very early in the spring when these same shoots are about 3 inches high. The aphids which sometimes appear may be killed by spraying with tobacco water.

COREOPSIS GRANDIFLORA. 3 feet. Sow in seedbed in early spring. Separate when the plants crowd each

Coreopsis grandiflora

other, and in the autumn transplant to the
borders or to rows in the garden for cutting.
A valuable bright yellow flower,—blooms
continuously, has long stems; quite hardy.

DELPHINIUM (Larkspur). 4 to 8 feet. Plant

Delphinium

in the fall. No manure should be allowed to come near the roots, but bone meal may be used in May, and coal-ashes should be sprinkled on the crown in the autumn as a preventive of the white grub which destroys the plant. Grows so high that it should always be staked. Larkspur is easily grown from seed, but should be finally set out,

Delphinium

where it is to bloom, by September 20th. Begins blooming the end of June, and if the stalks are cut down when the plant has finished blooming, a second, and often a third, crop of blossoms will be produced. There are often twelve to twenty stalks of blossoms on

229

a single plant. The plants should be given a little bone meal each time they are cut down. The larkspur has been wonderfully developed, and there are many varieties. The English catalogues mention over two hundred. These are tall- and low-growing, single and double, light blue and dark blue, blue and lavender, and all these shades combined.

DIANTHUS BARBATUS (Newport Pink; Sweet William). 1 to 2 feet. Considered a perennial, but it is wiser to sow fresh seed every year than to rely on dividing old plants. Sow the seed in the seed-bed in rows, in May, and, in July, transplant to about 6 to 8 inches apart. Finally, in the fall, by September 20th, transplant the little plants to the beds or borders where they are to bloom the following year. Blooms in June, for nearly a month. An old-time garden favorite, with straight, stiff stems and large heads of bloom, often five inches across. Individual flowers are often as large as a nickel. Sweet Williams make a beautiful edging for a border. It is a healthy plant, remains in bloom for fully three weeks, and the flowers are of beautiful colors—white, pink, crimson, yellow, white with a pink eye. Newport Pink, a new variety, is particularly beautiful, being a watermelon-pink. It does not, however, seem to be quite as hardy as the other varieties.

DICTAMNUS (Gas Plant). 2 to 3 feet. Plant in the spring in a sunny place. It should be seldom transplanted, but the roots may be separated. Blooms in June and July. In hot weather, the odd pink-and-white flowers give out a fragrant oil which a lighted match will ignite. The tall spikes of bloom make this a very handsome perennial.

DICENTRA (Bleeding Heart). 1 to 2 feet. Plant in the fall, as it starts very early in the spring. Blooms in May and June. The long racemes of heart-shaped pink-and-white flowers are familiar to all lovers of old-fashioned gardens.

DIGITALIS (Foxglove). 2 to 4 feet. Plant in the spring or fall. Sow the seed in April in

231

the seed-bed. Transplant about the middle of July into rows, 6 inches apart, and then transplant finally, not later than September 20th, to where the plants are to bloom the following year. Foxgloves often seed themselves, and the little plants thus seeded can be taken up and replanted in the spring. Blooms in June and July for about a month. One of the most beautiful and invaluable of all the perennials. Is white, pink, lavender and purple. The great spikes are a mass of hanging, bell-shaped flowers, and a row of them in a border is a beautiful sight.

ERYNGIUM (Sea Holly). 2 to 3 feet. Plant in the early spring or fall. Blooms from July. A large, decorative plant, suggestive of a thistle, with grey-green flowers. Excellent in shrubberies and wild gardens.

EUPATORIUM PURPUREUM. $1\frac{1}{2}$ to 4 feet. Plant in the spring or fall. Blooms from August until frost. A very healthy, useful plant. Good in borders or the wild garden. The flowers grow in clusters, and are white and, in the Purpureum, our native variety, purple.

FUNKIA SUBCORDATA and F. CŒRULEA (Plantain Lily; Day Lily). 1½ to 2 feet. Plant in the spring or fall. Should be rarely disturbed. Blooms in August and September. The broad, glossy foliage is very ornamental, and the white, or lilac, flowers are attractive. Does well in the sun but prefers partial shade.

Funkia

GAILLARDIA GRANDIFLORA (Blanket Flower). 2 feet. Plant in spring or autumn. Begins to bloom in June and continues all summer. A

most effective perennial, with flowers shading
from brown in the center through crimson and
orange to yellow on the edge of the petals.
It should be protected in winter.

GENTIANA ANDREWSII (Blue Gentian). 2
to 3 feet. Plant in the spring or fall. Blooms
in September. This familiar wood and meadow
flower is a deep, rich blue. Particularly good
in damp places.

GYPSOPHILA PANICULATA (Baby's Breath).
2 to 3 feet. Plant in the spring or fall. Blooms
in August and September. A mass of delicate,
tiny white flowers. Perhaps more graceful
and dainty than any other perennial.

GRASSES, ORNAMENTAL. 6 inches to 10 feet.
Plant in the spring or fall. All grasses need rich
soil and plenty of water. ERIANTHUS RAVENNÆ
(Plume Grass, or Hardy Pampas). GYNERIUM
ARGENTEUM (Pampas Grass). A very effective
grass with long, silvery plumes. PHALARIS
ARUNDINACEA VARIEGATA. Variegated Ribbon
Grass. UNIOLA LATIFOLIA (Spike Grass). One of
our finest and most ornamental native grasses.

HELIANTHUS MULTIFLORUS PLENUS (Hardy Sunflower). 4 to 8 feet. Plant in the spring or fall. Blooms from July to frost, according to the variety. An excellent perennial for shrubberies or large borders. The yellow flowers are both large and small, single and double.

HELIOPSIS (Orange Sunflower). 2 to 3 feet. Plant in the spring or fall. Begins blooming in July. Much like the Helianthus, but begins to bloom sooner, and, being smaller, is very good for cutting.

HELLEBORUS (Christmas Rose). 18 inches. Plant in the fall. Blooms in February and March. This plant is very satisfactory, as it gives many

Helleborus niger

THE PRACTICAL FLOWER GARDEN

large white blossoms when snow is on the ground.

HEMEROCALLIS FLAVA, FLORHAM and AURANTIACA (Yellow Day Lily). 1½ to 4 feet. Plant in the spring or fall. Blooms in June and July, according to the variety. Flava, perhaps the most familiar variety, has large, sweet, yellow flowers.

HEPATICA (Liver Leaf). 6 inches. Plant in the fall. Blooms in the earliest spring. Our native Hepatica has blue flowers; the cultivated varieties are white, red and purple. Lovely in shady places, along streams or ponds, and in woody corners.

HESPERIS MATRONALIS (Rocket). 2 to 4 feet. Plant in fall. Blooms in May and June. A strong, healthy perennial, much like a phlox. It is white, pink, lilac and purple, and quite fragrant. It increases rapidly.

HIBISCUS MOSCHEUTOS (Mallow). 3 to 4 feet. Plant in the spring or in the fall. Blooms in July and August. A very beautiful plant, easy to raise in moist places, but will succeed

236

in shrubberies and large borders if mulched and kept wet. The flowers are pale pink, deep pink with a deeper-colored eye, and white with a crimson eye.

HOLLYHOCK. 4 to 8 feet. Plant in the early spring. It can be easily raised from seed, which should be sown in rows early in April in the seed-bed, transplanted in July, about 8 inches apart, and then once more in September to where the plants are to bloom. Hollyhocks should be set out 2 feet apart. The plants must be sprayed with Bordeaux mixture as soon as they are up, and again about May 10th, and once more about June 1st, to prevent rust—an unsightly disease which much disfigures the leaves and finally causes them to drop off. A beautiful and highly decorative plant, with large, single and double flowers that grow along the stalk and are of many colors. It is invaluable for the back of a border.

INCARVILLEA (Hardy Gloxinia). 1½ to 2 feet. Plant in the early spring, in sun or shade, but should be covered in winter. Blooms in July and August. A very attractive new perennial. The rose-pink flowers grow in clusters and last a long time.

Japanese Iris

Iris. 2 to 3 feet. Plant all Iris in the fall, in rich, well-drained beds. They should be well mulched in summer and kept wet. In winter it is wise to use a slight covering.

I. KÆMPFERI (Japanese Iris). Blooms from the middle of June, for six weeks. One of the most wonderful of all garden flowers, and one which should never be omitted under any conditions. The great single and double flowers are white, violet, purple

238

and crimson. Some varieties are shaded and veined. No words can adequately describe their beauty. The roots increase and can be divided.

I. GERMANICA (German Iris). Another most beautiful and satisfactory variety, not as large as the Kæmpferi, but very desirable. Blooms from the end of May, for three weeks. It also increases and can be divided. The colors are yellow, white, mauve and purple, and many varieties combine two or more of these colors.

I. FLORENTINA (Florentine Iris). Blooms the end of May.

I. ANGLICA, MONT BLANC (English Iris). Blooms early in June. 3 feet.

I. SIBIRICA (Siberian Iris). 3 feet. Blooms in May. A small, delicate, rather tall-growing Iris that is purple and white, veined with mauve.

I. HISPANICA (Spanish Iris). 1 to 1½ feet. Blooms the middle of June. Many colors.

LAVANDULA (Lavender). 1½ to 2 feet. Plant in the spring or fall. Blooms in

July and August. The sweet lavender of our grandmothers, who used the dried flowers among their linen to give it fragrance. Pretty, but not particularly effective. Many who do not want to be without it grow it in the vegetable garden.

LIATRIS (Blazing Star; Gay Feather). 4 to 5 feet. Plant in the spring, or fall before October 15th. Blooms from July to September. An invaluable plant in the mixed border, for its tall spikes of purplish blue flowers are most effective.

LILIUM (Lily). Plant lilies in the early spring, or in October. They need well-drained, rich soil, and should be set out with a handful of sand around each bulb. They should be planted 8 to 18 inches deep, and be well covered in winter, and, if possible, mulched in summer. All but the *L. rubrum* do well in the sun, and look better in the border when planted in clumps of six or more. Beds of lilies, either of one variety or mixed, are very handsome.

L. AURATUM. Blooms from the middle of July, for one month. Perhaps the most beautiful and most fragrant lily. Will come up only a few years and then it is gone —why, no one seems to quite understand— but it is well worth having.

Lilium auratum

L. SPECIOSUM ALBUM. Blooms in June and July. Needs full sun. This lily can be separated about every three or four years. It must be planted in the fall, by October 15th.

L. CANADENSE (Meadow Lily). Plant in the spring, or in October. Will grow anywhere, but prefers a moist place. The flowers are yellow, red and orange. It increases very satisfactorily.

241

L. HANSONI. Blooms in June. A perfectly hardy, yellow Japanese lily.

L. LONGIFLORUM. Blooms early in July. Much like the Bermuda lily, but it is hardy.

L. TIGRINUM. Blooms in July and increases rapidly. The old-fashioned Tiger lily. By planting the little black bulbils that are found on the stalk, any number of bulbs can be procured.

L. SPECIOSUM RUBRUM. Blooms the end of August and early in September. A pink variety that thrives and increases; needs partial shade.

L. RUBELLUM. Blooms the middle of June. A pale pink lily.

L. KRAMERI. Blooms the middle of June.

L. BROWNII. Blooms the middle of July. A large lily, white inside and shaded on the outside with brown and purple.

L. WALLACEI. Blooms the end of July. A large, apricot-colored lily with brown spots.

L. BATEMANNI. Blooms the end of July. An apricot-colored lily without spots.

L. CHALCEDONICUM (Turk's Cap). Blooms the end of July. This lily grows in clusters and looks like a small tiger lily.

L. LEICHTLINI. Blooms in August. A Japanese lily that is pale yellow with purple markings.

L. SUPERBUM. Blooms all through August. A very healthy, free-blooming lily with crimson-orange flowers. Sometimes there will be as many as thirty flowers on one stalk.

L. MELPOMENE. Blooms middle of August. Much like the Rubrum but more brilliant in color.

LOBELIA CARDINALIS (Cardinal Flower; *Syphilitica hybrida*, Great Lobelia). 1 to 3 feet. Plant in the spring or fall. Needs a good, rich soil, and must be kept very wet. Blooms in August and September. The Cardinal Flower seen growing beside all mountain lakes and streams is a rich, fiery red, while the Great Lobelia has tall spikes of blue or white flowers. The blue is the best.

LYSIMACHIA CLETHROIDES (Loosestrife). 2 to 3 feet. Plant in the spring or fall. A very beautiful perennial with white or yellow flowers. The *L. clethroides* has tall, drooping spikes of small white flowers.

LUPINUS (Lupine). 2 to 4 feet. Plant in the spring or fall. Blooms the end of May, for three weeks. Needs good, rich soil and plenty of water. This perennial is easily raised from seed, which should be sown in mid-April after being soaked for twenty-four hours. It is very healthy and hardy. The tall spikes of blue, white or pink flowers are most effective, and quite invaluable in the borders.

LYCHNIS CHALCEDONICA (London Pride; Campion). 1 to 3 feet. Plant in the spring or fall. Very easy to grow, thriving in any soil. Blooms from June, according to variety. A popular hardy plant with white, rose or crimson flowers. The best-known variety, London Pride, blooms all summer and has vivid scarlet heads of bloom.

MONARDA DIDYMA (Oswego Tea) and ROSEA

(Bee Balm). (Bergamot.) 2 to 3 feet. Plant in the spring or fall. Thrives in any soil and in either sun or shade. Blooms in July and August. The odd flowers are crimson, rose-colored and white. Bee Balm is the old, familiar crimson variety.

MONTBRETIA. 1½ to 2 feet. Plant the bulbs in April and May, in clumps of twelve or more. Should be protected in winter. Blooms all summer. One of the most brilliant of our summer-flowering bulbs. The spikes of delicate flowers are yellow, orange and scarlet.

PEONIES, TREE. 2 to 4 feet. Plant in the spring or fall. Perfectly hardy, but should be somewhat pro-

Peony

245

tected in winter, and, as they start early, should be manured in the fall. Bloom from the middle of May. The flowers are rose and white, and some varieties are variegated.

P. JAPANESE SINGLE. 2 to 3½ feet. Plant in the fall. Bloom in May and June. Even more beautiful than the ordinary double peony.

P., DOUBLE HERBACEOUS. 3 to 4 feet. Plant in the fall, so that the crown is covered with about 3 inches of soil. A good, rich soil and a sunny place, with plenty of water while the buds are forming, will make them magnificent. They will, however, thrive under any conditions, for they are very hardy, healthy and quite free from pests of any kind. All peonies

Papaver orientale. See page 247.

should be manured in the fall, as they start very early. When once planted, peonies should rarely, if ever, be disturbed. Bloom in May and June. The best and most beautiful of all spring flowers. Better in masses, or in rows, than as individual plants.

PAPAVER ORIENTALE (Oriental Poppy). 2 to 4 feet. Plant in early spring, or fall, in almost any soil. With occasional watering, and a mulch in the fall, this plant will thrive and increase greatly in size, and the roots may be divided. Blooms in May and June. Far surpassing all other poppies in size and brilliancy of color. It is scarlet and pink. Can easily be raised from seed.

P. NUDICAULE (Iceland Poppy). 1 to 2 feet. Plant in the spring or fall. Blooms all summer. Bright green, fern-like foliage, and delicate white, yellow, orange and scarlet flowers. A pretty, healthy plant, easy to grow.

PHLOX. Many varieties. 3 to 4 feet. Plant 18 inches apart, in the fall, from October 1st to 15th, or in earliest spring. Needs a rich soil. Plenty of watering increases the size of the blossoms. Every three years, each plant should be lifted, separated into bunches of from three to four stalks each, and reset. The mildew which attacks the leaves in moist summers can be arrested by a dusting of powdered sulphur, or by spraying with Bordeaux mixture. Phlox will bloom from June until frost if both early and late varieties are chosen, and if the heads are cut off as soon as they have finished blooming. One of the most satisfactory of all perennials, and absolutely indispensable to the hardy garden. It would be almost impossible to have too many plants, as there are so many varieties and the range of colors is so great— white, white with pink and red and purple eyes, all the shades of pink from rose to cherry, scarlet and red, combinations of rose and red, purple and combinations of purple and many mottled varieties. By breaking off the flower-heads as soon as they have bloomed, a second crop will often be produced.

P. SUBULATA (Moss, or Mountain Pink).
6 inches. Plant in the fall. Blooms in early
spring. The pretty evergreen foliage is quite
hidden in blooming-time by a mass of color—
rose, lilac and white. Good for the rock-garden.

PHYSOSTEGIA (False Dragonhead). 3 to 4
feet. Plant in the spring or fall. Blooms in
July and August. A very beautiful perennial,
with great spikes of pink-and-white bloom.

PENTSTEMON BARBATUS TORREYI, and P.
DIGITALIS (Beard Tongue). 2 to 4 feet. Plant
in the early spring, or between October 1st and
15th. Blooms from June to September. The
tall spikes of bloom are white, red and blue.
The *P. barbatus Torreyi* is perhaps the most
beautiful variety. Its spikes of flowers are a
brilliant scarlet. It blooms in June and July.
The *P. digitalis* has long heads of white flowers. It increases rapidly and is very effective.

PLATYCODON MARIESI (Balloon Flower; Japanese Bellflower). 2 to 3 feet. Plant in the
spring. Needs good soil and covering in winter. Blooms from the middle of July, for six

weeks. A beautiful perennial, not widely
known. The blue or white cup-shaped flowers
are like little balloons when in bud. It is not
attacked by pests and is very healthy; has

Platycodon

often nearly a hundred blossoms on one
plant, and is easily raised from seed.

PYRETHRUM. 3 to 5 feet. Plant in good
soil in the spring or fall. Must have full sun.
Blooms in June and again in September. A
very fine perennial, with great daisy-like
flowers in crimson, white and pink. Can be
raised from seed.

RUDBECKIA, GOLDEN GLOW (Cone Flower).

4 to 8 feet. Plant in the fall or early spring. An absolutely hardy, healthy perennial that will grow in any soil. Useful as a screen or in the back of a border. Must be staked. It increases tremendously, and is good for cutting. It should be divided in October. Spraying with tobacco water will kill the aphids that sometimes attack this plant. There are several varieties—some with yellow, others with purple flowers. The best-known variety, Golden Glow, is in blooming-time a mass of deep yellow blossoms, like small, double sunflowers.

SALVIA GRANDIFLORA AZUREA. Can be raised from seed sown when the ground is warm, and also increased by separating the roots. Plant grows from two to three feet high, and is covered, in August and September, with open clusters of light blue flowers. The plants need winter protection; in cold localities, the coldframe is advisable for the first year.

SCABIOSA CAUCASICA and S. ALBA. $1\frac{1}{4}$ to $2\frac{1}{2}$ feet. Plant in the spring or fall,

localities and storing them in sand in a cool cellar. It is effective in borders and also in masses, either in beds or in front of other taller-growing plants. Is easily raised from seed.

VALERIANA COCCINEA ALBA (White Valerian). 2 to 3 feet. Plant in the fall, before October 15th, for it starts very early. Blooms in May and June. An attractive, fragrant perennial, excellent in a white border. The tall-growing heads of bloom are a great addition to an old-time garden.

VERONICA LONGIFOLIA SUBSESSILIS (Speedwell). 1 to 3 feet. Plant in the spring, that it may become well established before winter. A beautiful blue perennial, blooming, from the middle of July, for a month. Plants three years old bear eight to ten tall spikes of blossoms; needs a good soil and plenty of watering; is very healthy and quite hardy if covered in winter.

VINCA (Periwinkle, or Trailing Myrtle). 6 inches. Plant in the spring. Blooms in midsummer. A trailing evergreen plant, with

star-like blue flowers. Can be planted with
success wherever grass will not grow—in very
shady places, around the roots of trees or on
steep slopes.

VIOLET, HARDY. 6 inches to 1 foot. Plant
in the spring, or fall before October 15.
Blooms in early May. Our native white and
purple violet—also a pretty yellow one—is
an attractive, early-blooming flower for the
border, or along streams or ponds.

WALLFLOWER. 1 foot. Plant in the spring
or fall. Blooms in June. One of the oldest
perennials, always associated with our grandmothers' gardens. The pretty brown, yellow-
and maroon-colored flowers are familiar to
many.

YUCCA FILAMENTOSA (Adam's Needle). 3 to
4 feet. Plant in the spring. Blooms in July.
A Mexican desert plant, and one of the most
effective in the garden. The great spikes of
bell-like, creamy white flowers, resembling
orchids, are unequaled for effectiveness. It
seems to prefer a very dry, sunny place, and

hence will succeed where few other plants are satisfactory. It should be somewhat covered in winter, as a late spring frost is apt to kill the flower stalk, which starts very early. It is otherwise perfectly hardy and healthy, needing no water or fertilizer.

ANNUALS

ACROCLINIUM (Everlasting). $1\frac{1}{4}$ to $1\frac{1}{2}$ feet. Sow the seed early in spring, and transplant later to where it is to bloom. Blooms from early in July. This plant blossoms profusely and has a wide variety of colors. White and pale pink are the best.

AGERATUM (Floss Flower). 1 to $1\frac{1}{2}$ feet. Sow the seed in a hotbed in March. Transplant to the open ground in May, or sow the seed outdoors in May and transplant later. Blooms from early in July until late fall, if the dead flowers are cut off. Perhaps the most satisfactory blue bedding-out plant. The feathery blossoms grow in such profusion that the foliage is often quite hidden. It is white and several shades of blue, but as a blue flower it is eminently successful

ALOYSIA CITRIODORA (Lemon Verbena). 8 inches to 2 feet. Plant out-of-doors in May. Can be started from cuttings, or small plants can be bought from any nurseryman. The pretty, very fragrant leaves are familiar to all, and can be put to many uses.

ALYSSUM (Madwort). 4 to 8 inches. Sow the seed in May where it is to bloom. Blooms almost all summer. A most satisfactory flower for edging borders. Its delicate clusters of sweet-scented, tiny white flowers make a good frame for the larger, handsomer and showier flowers.

ANTIRRHINUM (Snapdragon). 1 to 2½ feet. Some sow the seed for early blooming in the fall and cover lightly during the winter, but this can be done safely only in rather mild climates. In cold localities, it is better to start snapdragon in hotbeds in March and transfer to the open ground in May. It needs a rich soil and a sunny situation.

257

Blooms from July until frost, if the dead flowers are kept cut. A wonderful flower, just beginning to be appreciated. There is no annual that more repays the gardener in effectiveness. The tall spikes of bloom are sturdy and healthy, and are one mass of the odd little flowers that give the plant its name. It comes in many colors—deep crimson, deep yellow, and wonderful orange-brown tones, but the creamy whites and pale pinks are, perhaps, the most enchanting.

ASTER, CHRYSANTHEMUM-FLOWERED, BRANCHING PEONY-FLOWERED, OSTRICH FEATHER, and AMERICAN. 1 to 3 feet. For early blooming, sow the seeds in a coldframe in April. For late blooming, sow in May, in the open ground. When the seedlings have two leaves, transplant them nine to twelve inches apart, where they are to bloom. They should have rich soil. A little wood-ashes is a good fertilizer. A sure method of destroying the black beetles that infest the blossoms is to pick them off, one at a time, and drop them into a convenient pan of kerosene. Early varieties begin blooming in July, and, by judicious sowing, a succession of flowers can be had until frost. There is no more satisfactory annual and none that better repays cultivation. The new varieties are wonderful in the size and fullness of the heads. The names of the different varieties quite describe them. Particularly attractive are the Comet, a large, white, branch-

Aster, Ostrich Plume

ing aster, and the Daybreak, an exquisite shell-pink American aster. Purity, another American aster, is snow-white.

BALSAM, DOUBLE CAMELLIA-FLOWERED

259

(~~Lady's Slipper~~). 2 feet. Sow the seed indoors
in April; outdoors in May. Transplant to 18
inches apart. Blooms in July and August.
The old-fashioned garden flower in modern
perfection. In blooming-time, the plant is
one mass of scarlet, pink or white flowers,
from root to tip, the delicate green leaves
showing between the blossoms.

BEGONIA, TUBEROUS-ROOTED. 6 to 8 inches.
Plant in the hotbed for early blooming,
and in the open ground, in May, for blossoming in August. Plant with the hollow end
of the bulb uppermost, and cover with two
inches of soil. It prefers partial shade, but,
well mulched, is quite contented in the full
sun. The bulbs should be well dried and
stored in a cellar in winter. It has large,
rough leaves and great, single, double and
frilled, many-colored flowers; is a plant suitable to use as a carpet under lilies, iris and
other narrow-leaved flowers.

CALENDULA (Pot Marigold). 1 to $1\frac{1}{2}$ feet.
Sow the seed in May where it is to bloom—

preferably a sunny place. Blooms in August and September—until frost. The marigold of Shakspere's time in many modern varieties—both single and double. It comes in all the oranges and yellows, and many varieties are striped and shaded.

CALLIOPSIS. $1\frac{1}{2}$ to 2 feet. Sow the seed where it is to bloom in early spring, and, later, thin out to from eight to twelve inches apart. Blooms the end of July or August. The delicate, ragged, yellow flowers, with dark centers, grow on tall, slim stems and are very dainty and attractive.

CANDYTUFT. 6 inches. Sow the seed in April where it is to bloom. Blooms in June. A mass of small white flowers; very good for edging beds and borders.

CANNA. 3 to 8 feet. Plant the roots either in the hotbed in April or in the open ground in May. Blooms from July until frost. No other bedding-out plant is more satisfactory. The tall spikes of bloom, either red or yellow, or the two colors combined, and the large,

smooth, green leaves make it exceedingly
decorative. It can be used in masses, or a few
plants can be scattered through the borders.
The roots must be stored indoors in winter;
they will be found to increase tremendously.

CARNATION, MARGUERITE, PERPETUAL. 1
to 1½ feet. Sow the seed in May, in rich
soil. Transplant in September to where it is
to bloom the following spring. The plants
should be set 8 inches apart, and must be
kept well watered. In winter some covering
should be used. For early flowering, start the
plants in the hotbeds, and transfer in May
to the open ground, where they will begin to
bloom in a few weeks. The blossoms are
double, very sweet, and of good size. They
come in almost all colors and in many combinations of color.

CELOSIA CRISTATA PLUMOSA (Coxcomb). 2
to 4 feet. Sow indoors in April and transplant
in May to where it will bloom, or sow outdoors in May. It does not require rich soil.
Blooms from July until frost. A large, showy

plant, with flowers at the end of every branch. They are a rich crimson and a good yellow. In some varieties the combs attain an enormous size. In the Plumosa the flower is more feathery and graceful.

CENTAUREA CYANUS (Cornflower; Ragged Sailor; Bachelor's Button; Kaiser Blume). 3 to 4 feet. Sow in early spring where it is to bloom. Blooms from June until frost if not allowed to go to seed. This familiar flower, with its beautiful blue color, comes in both single and double varieties, and can also be had in white and pink. After it is once established it will often seed itself and come up, from its own seeding, year after year.

C. IMPERIALIS (Royal Sweet Sultan). 2 feet. Sow the seed in very early spring. Blooms the end of July and August. The flowers resemble delicate, dainty thistles, are purple, lilac, rose and white, and are excellent for combination with other flowers in house decoration.

COLEUS (Flame Nettle). 1 foot. Sow the

seed indoors in March. Transplant in May to open ground. A favorite bedding-plant with variegated leaves.

COSMOS, MAMMOTH PERFECTION, LADY LENOX and EXTRA EARLY. 5 to 10 feet. Sow as early as possible in the open ground or

under cover. Transplant to 18 inches apart. Does better in a light soil and should be staked. Blooms from the end of July until frost. This almost shrub-like plant has a profusion of daisy-like flowers that are

Cosmos

white, pink, lavender, yellow and crimson. White Cosmos is probably the most beautiful. In localities where frost comes early, it is wiser to buy only the early-flowering varieties, otherwise the plants will be killed just as they are ready to bloom.

DAHLIA, CACTUS, DECORATIVE, GIANT, PON-PON, COLLARETTE, QUILL, SINGLE CENTURY, SINGLE and PEONY-FLOWERED. 2 to 8 feet. Plant the dormant roots in good, rich soil as early as possible in the spring, preferably in a sunny place. Set out about three feet apart and allow only one shoot to grow, which should be thoroughly staked and well watered. The roots should be dried and stored indoors in winter. They increase greatly. The many varieties and wonderful colors of the modern dahlia make it a totally different flower from the one our grandmothers knew. The names are descriptive of the different varieties, and as there are so many of them, and they bloom from early in June or July until frost, a garden of dahlias might be very interesting. There is great pleasure in saving and planting one's own seed. The results are most instructive and often surprising.

DIANTHUS CHINENSIS (Annual Pink). 6 to 18 inches. Sow the seed as early as possible in the spring. It begins to bloom a few weeks from the time of sowing and continues blossoming profusely until frost. If slightly covered, it will often survive the winter and bloom again the next spring. The flowers, single and double, come in almost all colors and in many combinations of color. They have that delightful cinnamon odor, so suggestive of an old-time garden.

ESCHSCHOLTZIA (California Poppy). 6 to 12 inches. Sow the seed very thinly in early spring where it is to grow. Blooms all summer. Useful in masses, for edging beds, or for planting in the rock-garden. The colors are white, pink, yellow, orange and scarlet.

GLADIOLI. 2 to 3 feet. The bulbs need a good, rich soil and, preferably, a sunny place. They should be staked when a foot high, and in winter must be stored indoors. By a succession of plantings, beginning in early May, continual bloom can be had from July until frost. This most beautiful and satisfactory summer-flowering bulb should always find a place in the garden. It is effective in masses, or as single plants in the borders of rose- and lily-beds. The tall spikes of bloom and the iris-like leaves are very decorative. The modern gladiolus is much like an orchid in shape and in the many wonderful colors in which it is produced. Some of the flowers are often three inches across, and no words can describe the marvelous colors.

GODETIA. 1 foot. Sow the seed in early spring and transplant later to a foot apart. Prefers a rather poor soil and partial shade. Blooms from July until September. An attractive annual with many delicate poppy-like flowers that are white, red or pink. Good as a border to flower-beds.

GERANIUM (Pelargonium). 1 to 1½ feet. Start the dormant roots, or slips, in March, indoors, or plant them in the open ground in May. Blooms from June until frost. A popular bedding-out plant; good for terrace or piazza decoration. The flowers, single or double, are red, pink and white. The leaves are round and furry, and, in some cases, variegated. Some varieties are fragrant, such as the rose and lemon geranium.

HELIANTHUS (Sunflower). 3 to 10 feet. Sow the seeds in April or May in a sunny place. Blooms from July until frost. Another old garden flower which is a rich, glowing yellow. Some sunflowers are of great size, others, and perhaps the most attractive, are quite small.

HELIOTROPE. 1 to 1½ feet. Sow the seed in the greenhouse very early in the spring, or start in greenhouse from slips and transplant later where it is to bloom. It needs a rich soil and plenty of sun. Blooms from the first of July until frost, and is a very fragrant and beautiful blue-purple flower. In warm climates it lives out-of-doors all winter and grows as large as an ordinary shrub. An excellent bedding-out plant, as it is a mass of rich color through most of the summer.

HYACINTHUS CANDICANS (Cape Hyacinth). 3 to 5 feet. Plant the bulb in bed or border in early spring. Blooms in July and August. A beautiful white summer-flowering bulb, with tall spikes of drooping hyacinth-like flowers. Quite invaluable. The bulbs are hardy and should remain in the ground in winter.

ISMENE CALATHINA (Peruvian Daffodil). 1½ to 2 feet. Plant the bulbs in the open beds in spring. Blooms in August. A little-known, but beautiful summer-blooming bulb. It has great, queer, white, lily-shaped flowers; very interesting and attractive. The bulbs should be stored in winter.

KOCHIA (Standing Cypress). 1 to 3 feet. Sow the seed in spring and transplant into rows about a foot apart. A pyramidal-shaped plant with fine, feathery foliage that in summer is a light, delicate green; later the whole plant becomes a brilliant red. Very good for a little hedge around the seed-bed or the vegetable garden.

269

MARIGOLD, AFRICAN and FRENCH. 2 to 4 feet. Sow the seed in early spring and transplant, when four inches high, to where it will bloom. Blooms from August until frost. A most decorative annual, with its handsome cut leaf and its many large ball- or daisy-shaped flowers, that are either a rich lemon-yellow or a deep orange. No flower is easier to grow, but, as it has a very pungent odor, many do not care for it near the house or for indoor decoration.

MIGNONETTE (Reseda). 6 to 12 inches. Sow the seed in early spring and again in July. Blooms by such successive sowing from June until frost. It needs a rich soil. An old-fashioned garden never seems quite complete without this fragrant flower of our grandmother's time. The spikes of delicate green and white bloom combine well with other flowers. It is not difficult to grow.

MYOSOTIS (Forget-me-not). 6 to 12 inches. Sow the seed where it is to bloom. Blooms in June. Is perennial in some localities if covered in the winter. It thrives in moist, shady places. The popular flower of song and story, with silvery green leaves and little blue, star-like flowers.

NASTURTIUM, DWARF and CLIMBING VARIETIES. Sow the seed where it is to bloom —preferably a sunny place. Blooms from July until frost. The blossoms come in almost all colors, plain and variegated, are very delicate and suggest a fairy's peaked cap. The light green leaves are nearly round and very prettily veined. It thrives almost

Nasturtium

271

anywhere and responds to the slightest care. In fact, no other annual is so very easy to grow.

NICOTIANA AFFINIS and SANDERÆ HYBRIDS (Tuberose-flowered Tobacco). 2 to 3 feet. Sow seeds in early spring. Blooms from July until frost. The sweet-scented white flowers of these fall annuals are very attractive against a dark background of shrubs.

NIGELLA (Love-in-a-Mist). 1 foot. Sow seeds in early spring. A free-blooming annual. The curious-looking flowers are blue and white.

ŒNOTHERA (Evening Primrose). 3 feet. Sow the seed in spring and transplant to a sunny place. Blooms in July and August. The large yellow, white and pink flowers remain closed during the day, opening wide after sundown.

PANSY. 6 to 12 inches. Sow the seed in drills. Cover very lightly with rich soil. Transplant to a sunny place, 8 inches apart. Seed can be sown in August, transplanted in

September and kept covered all winter. The
August-sown seed will bloom the middle of
the following May, and seed sown in April
will bloom the end of June. This familiar
flower is good for borders, around flower-
beds, or as a carpet with tall-growing plants.
There are many varieties.

PETUNIA, DOUBLE LARGE-FLOWERING,
SINGLE LARGE-FLOWERING, SINGLE BED-
DING and ROSY MORN. 1 to 1½ feet. The
seed should be sown indoors and transplanted
to the open ground in May. Blooms from
June. Wholly unlike the old-fashioned petunia.
The flowers are of great size, single or double.
Many varieties are fringed, and come in the
most beautiful colors. It is a revelation to
see what the hybridizer has done with a plain,
old-fashioned, and rather unpopular, flower.

PHLOX DRUMMONDII. 6 to 12 inches. Sow
seed in the open ground as soon as all danger
of frost is past. Transplant later to where they
are to bloom. Blooms continuously from a
few weeks after the seed is sown until frost.

Really a dwarf annual phlox. Color, white, pink, lilac, scarlet and crimson. Effective as an edging for beds or a carpet under taller-growing plants.

PAPAVER, SINGLE ANNUAL and DOUBLE ANNUAL (Poppy). 8 inches to 2 feet. Sow the seed in early spring and thin out the plants to from 3 to 4 inches apart. Blooms in July. A bed of annual poppies in full bloom is most effective in the garden. The large and small, single and double flowers come in many exquisite colors, and it is difficult to decide which are most beautiful—the great, ragged, double ones or the delicate single flowers with their large centers.

PORTULACA (Sunplant). 6 inches. Sow the seed where it is to grow. Blooms all summer. A very healthy, easily-grown annual that loves a sunny place. Profusely covered with red, yellow, white, pink or variegated flowers. Good to plant in the rock-garden.

RICHARDIA (Calla). 2 to 3 feet. Plant the bulb in May in the open border or bed.

Should be staked. Blooms in August. Familiar as a greenhouse plant but not usually seen in gardens. It is, however, very attractive, and when used, like gladiolus and tuberoses, among roses, or in the lily beds, will be found satisfactory. The bulbs should be stored in winter.

RICINUS (Castor-Oil Bean). 8 feet. Sow seed early in the spring. Great ornamental plants with large reddish green leaves and red fruit. Decorative in shrubberies or against buildings.

SALPIGLOSSIS (Painted Tongue). 1½ to 2 feet. Sow seed in hotbed and transplant to the open ground in May. Blooms from July until frost. The flowers of this annual are delicate, attractive and suggestive of an orchid. They come in various colors—purple and gold, rose and gold, scarlet and gold, white and gold. The petals of the flowers are one color and the deep veining another.

SALVIA, BONFIRE (Scarlet Sage). 3 feet. Sow in the hotbed in February. Transplant

in May to where it is to bloom. Blooms from
middle of July until frost. Sometimes considered a perennial, but will not survive
the winter in our northern climate. A very
beautiful and popular bright red flower that
looks equally well in masses or as a single
plant in a red border.

S. PATENS (Blue Sage or Salvia). 2 to $2\frac{1}{2}$
feet. Sow in the hotbed in the early spring
and transplant to where it is to bloom. Blooms
from July. No other flower in the garden
is of quite the same rich, brilliant blue;
is somewhat the shape of the red salvia
blossom, and grows around a spike about five
inches long. Unlike the delphinium, in
which the whole spike blooms at once, only a
few scattered flowers blossom at a time;
is nevertheless an attractive plant. Sometimes considered hardy, but will not survive very cold winters and should always be
protected in winter.

SCHIZANTHUS (Butterfly Flower). 2 feet.
Sow the seed in early spring in a sheltered

corner. Blooms a few weeks from the time of sowing. One of the most dainty and delicate of all garden flowers. When in bloom, the whole plant is one mass of blossoms, orchid-like in shape and of many beautiful colors. It can never fail to please even the most difficult gardener.

STOCK (Gilliflower). 2 feet. Sow the seed in the hotbed for early blooming or in the open ground in May for later flowering. Blooms from July. One of the most beautiful annuals and should never be omitted from the garden. It is another of the old-time flowers that have come down from our grand-mothers' days. It has a delicate fragrance and the richness of the colors is always a delight to the eye. The deep yellow, deep red, deep purple, orange and browns are very fine. But the white and delicate shell-pink are perhaps the most satisfying.

SWEET PEAS. 4 feet. Sow the seed as early as possible in rich, loamy soil—preferably in a trench. Cover the seeds very lightly with

277

earth, hilling up as the plants grow, and thin the plants out to 2 inches apart. Must be kept well watered or the plants will shrivel and stop blossoming; all dead flowers and seed-pods should be kept cut for the same reason. Sweet peas should be staked with brush, or, better still, chicken-wire can be stretched for them to climb on, and is more tidy looking. Do not plant sweet peas in the same place too many years in succession. Begin to bloom the end of June and continue indefinitely. No more beautiful and satisfactory flower for indoor decoration. As they are better for that purpose when separated as to color, the wise

Sweet Peas

gardener will not buy mixed seeds but will buy and plant each variety by itself, and avoid the tiresome task of sorting the flowers according to color before putting them into vases. They come in every possible color and variation of color. But the white, rose and deep pink, lavender, deep maroon and deep purple will be found very beautiful.

TUBEROSE. 2 to 3 feet. Plant in the open border in May. Blooms in August and September. The bulb bears a very fragrant stalk of white bloom. It can be used in the same way as gladioli, callas or other tall-growing summer bulbs and, like them, should be staked and the bulb stored indoors in winter.

VERBENA. 1 to 1½ feet. Sow the seed in the hotbed and transplant to where it is to bloom in May. Blooms from early in June. The modern grower has so perfected this familiar flower, in its size and many beautiful colors, that it can hardly be recognized. The pale pink verbena is the most pleasing variety and is frequently used for bedding.

XERANTHEMUM (Everlasting, or Immortelle). 3 feet. Sow in May in the open ground. Blooms from July until frost. Bears a quantity of white, pink, purple and red blossoms.

ZINNIA. 2 feet. Sow early in the hotbeds, or in May, in the open ground. Blooms from July. One of the healthiest and most brilliant annuals, and useful to fill out the borders and give them color in late summer. The colors are white, scarlet, yellow, orange and salmon-pink. The latter is perhaps the most desirable shade because, after July, there are so few light-colored flowers in the garden.

HARDY VINES

AMPELOPSIS LOWII. Plant in the spring. A vine of the same characteristics as *Ampelopsis Veitchi*, but the foliage is smaller and deeper cut, giving to the vine a greater air of delicacy.

A. QUINQUEFOLIA (Virginia Creeper, or American Ivy). Plant in the spring, or transplant from the wild. The familiar five-leaved vine that grows on all roadside fences and walls. It has clusters of small purple berries in the fall and is very hardy. It must be trained, for, unlike *Ampelopsis Veitchi*, it does not cling sufficiently. Good on wooden houses, walls and rustic work.

A. Veitchi (Japan, or Boston Ivy). Plant in the spring. Very satisfactory against wood or stone, for it clings closely with its many tiny feet.

Bignonia grandiflora (Trumpet Creeper). Plant in the spring. Blooms from July. A perfectly hardy vine of rapid growth. It has clusters of large, orange-red, trumpet-shaped flowers, and its dense foliage makes it an excellent screen.

Celastrus Scandens (Bittersweet). Plant in the spring, or transplant from fields or woods. The well-known wild vine with clusters of sweet white flowers in the spring and, in the fall, beautiful orange-colored berries that, after frost, burst their outer orange coat, revealing the scarlet fruit.

CLEMATIS HENDERSONI, HENRYI and JACK-
MANI. Plant in the spring. Blooms in July.
A most beautiful vine of slow growth. It has

large star-shaped flow-
ers, white, as in Henryi,
or a deep purple, as in
Jackmani. Other varie-
ties are lavender, rose
and carmine.

C. PANICULATA,
FLAMMULA and VIR-
GINIANA (Japanese
Virgin's Bower). Plant
in the spring, or trans-
plant the common Vir-
giniana from the fields
and woods. Blooms in
August and September.

Clematis Jackmani

A very hardy, quick-growing, most satisfactory vine which, in blooming time, is a solid
mass of small white flowers.

DOLICHOS JAPONICUS (Kudzu Vine). Plant
in the spring. Blooms in August. It has

racemes of purplish pink, pea-like blossoms. Is the most rapid-growing vine in cultivation, often growing 30 feet in a year.

EUONYMUS RADICANS. Evergreen. Plant in the spring. A very hardy, slow-growing vine with small, smooth, regular leaves, either dark green or variegated green and white. It clings closely to stone, wood and the bark of trees.

HEDERA HELIX (English Ivy). Evergreen. Plant in the spring. The familiar vine with irregular leaves. Excellent for planting around stone houses or as a border around flower-beds, fountains or terraces. Not hardy north of central New Jersey unless covered in winter.

HUMULUS (Hop Vine). Plant in the spring. Blooms in June and July. Of rapid growth and quite hardy. Very useful as a screen. The racemes of pale green, odd-looking flowers are followed by seed-pods which can be put to many uses.

LONICERA (Honeysuckle). Plant in the spring. Blooms all summer. A familiar vine with white, yellow, pink or variegated flowers, and, in some varieties, variegated leaves. Very fragrant, absolutely hardy, and a good grower.

POLYGONUM MULTIFLORUM. Plant in the spring. Blooms in September and October. The flowers are tiny and white and cover the vine in great trusses of bloom. The leaves are large and heart-shaped. It is a strong, quick grower. Quite a new vine.

VITIS LABRUSCA and V. RIPARIA (Fox Grape; Frost Grape). Plant in the spring, or transplant from the wild. Blooms in June. The tiny fragrant flowers become, in the fall, clusters of small, dark blue, rather bitter grapes. The large leaves make it a very ornamental vine. It is absolutely hardy.

WISTARIA SINENSIS and W. SINENSIS ALBA (Chinese Wistaria). Plant in the spring. Blooms in May and June. When in full bloom there is no more beautiful vine. The huge pendent racemes of purple or white flowers so cover the entire plant that it is a wonderful, solid mass of color. It is very slow in starting but lives to a great age.

CLIMBING ROSES

RAMBLER ROSE, CRIMSON, LADY GAY, YEL-
LOW, WHITE and PINK DOROTHY PERKINS.
Plant in the spring, or by October 15th.
Blooms end of June and July. No more
beautiful hardy flowering vine. In blooming
time the huge clusters of small roses—either
crimson, cerise-pink, soft shell-pink, white or
yellow—are a joy to behold. They, and all
other climbing roses, must be trained and
tied, for they do not cling.

PRAIRIE QUEEN. Plant in early spring or
by October 15th. Blooms in July. Very
hardy. Blossoms of a deep rose color.

BALTIMORE BELLE. Plant in the spring, or
in fall not later than October 15th. Blooms
in June. The blush-pink blossoms of this
rose grow in clusters as in the Ramblers.

ANNUAL VINES

COBÆA SCANDENS (Cup-and-Saucer Vine).
Sow the seed edgewise in the spring and just

cover with soil. Blooms all summer. A very quick grower which easily clings to any rough surface, such as trunks of trees and trellises. The bell-shaped flowers are purple or white.

CONVOLVULUS (Morning Glory). Sow in the early spring. Soak the seeds in warm water over night before sowing. Blooms almost all summer; the familiar, wide-mouthed, trumpet flowers of many beautiful colors and of both single and double varieties.

ECHINOCYSTIS (Wild Cucumber Vine). Sow seed in early spring. Blooms all summer. One of the quickest-growing annual vines,— sometimes 25 feet in a summer. It has small yellow-white flowers.

IPOMŒA GRANDIFLORA (Moonflower). (Japanese Morning Glory.) Sow the seed in spring after the weather is settled; they should be soaked in warm water over night. Blooms all summer. It has very beautiful flowers, surpassing all other morning glories. Besides being a rapid grower, it is easy to cultivate. The white, fragrant flowers of the moonflower are five to six inches in diameter and appear at night and on dull days.

ORNAMENTAL GOURD. Sow the seed early in spring. Blooms through July and August, and then bears the many-shaped fruits from which the vine gets its name. This vine has been known to grow as much as a foot in a day.

SPRING-FLOWERING BULBS

CONVALLARIA MAJALIS (Lily-of-the-Valley). 8 inches. Plant in the fall, in clumps, in the sun, in shady places, along streams or in wooded corners. It increases tremendously. Blooms in May and June. A very popular spring-flowering bulb which is exceedingly healthy and hardy. The delicate, white, bell-like flowers are

Crocus

most fragrant, and the broad, smooth, green leaves decorative.

CROCUS. 4 to 5 inches. Plant in the fall, two inches apart, three inches deep, in good, rich ground. It should not be disturbed for several years; therefore it is often a good plan to plant it in the grass. Blooms the end of March and first of April, in many colors— white, yellow, purple, and some varieties are striped. A very popular bulb.

ERYTHRONIUM. (Dog's Tooth Violet.) 4 inches. Plant in the fall in any light soil. Blooms in April. These pretty yellow violets can be planted in groups in rockeries or in any sheltered

Narcissus, Emperor

place. Very satisfactory in the borders of shrubbery.

FRITILLARIA IMPERIALIS (Crown Imperial). 2 feet. Plant in the fall. Thrives in a rich, well-drained soil. Blooms in April or May. A tall-growing plant with dark green leaves and large, effective flowers in all the shades of red and yellow.

GALANTHUS NIVALIS (Snowdrop). 6 inches. Plant in the fall, 2 to 3 inches deep, in a shady place. Blooms very early in the spring, often before the snow is off the ground. The single varieties bloom first; the double varieties later.

HYACINTH. 1 foot. Plant in October in a light soil and a sunny place. If the soil is heavy, some sand will be useful, and if other plants have been in the bed all summer, some well-rotted manure should be used. Plant the bulbs six inches deep to the bottom of the bulb, and six to seven inches apart. The bulbs must be planted evenly or they will not bloom at the same time. It is well to plant each bulb in a handful of sand, to insure good drainage. A slight covering after the ground is frozen is beneficial. Blooms in May. One of the most popular of the spring-flowering bulbs. It is very fragrant and comes in many colors—blue, white, red, crimson, pink, lilac, mauve, yellow and orange. There are also both single and double varieties, but the single flowers are more graceful and often healthier.

JONQUIL. 1 foot. Plant in the fall. Treat in the same way as hyacinths. Blooms the

end of April and May. A plant related to the narcissus. The clusters of delicate yellow flowers are most attractive.

MUSCARI (Grape, Nutmeg or Feathered Hyacinth). 1 foot. Plant in the fall,

Narcissus, Sulphur Phœnix
See page 291

either in beds or boxes. Will thrive in any soil and needs little care. Can be naturalized in the grass. Blooms in May. The delicate, pretty flowers are most attractive. This will be found a generally useful bulb.

NARCISSUS, SULPHUR PHŒNIX, VON SION, ORNATUS, POETICUS, EMPEROR, EMPRESS and GOLDEN SPUR. 1 to 1½ feet. Plant in the fall in rows in beds or in the grass.

Narcissus, Von Sion

Will thrive in almost any soil or place. Increases, and should not be disturbed for years. It seems to prefer a good soil and a partially shaded place. Blooms in April and May. No flowers are more graceful and attractive.

291

Their charm is known to all, and the poetry of all ages has sung their beauty. There

Narcissus Ornatus

292

are single and double narcissi and daffodils, and there are white, yellow and the shades of yellow, or yellow and white. There is also a double white narcissus, which is particularly lovely. All these can be grown in the grass, in the wild garden, among shrubs and trees, or in wooded corners.

SCILLA. 8 inches. Plant in the fall. Almost all varieties are quite hardy and may remain untouched in the ground for years. Blooms in April. Some scillas are white and rose, but the familiar variety is a deep, rich blue, which makes a beautiful contrast with the

Narcissus Poeticus. See page 291

293

snowdrop and the crocus that bloom at the same time.

TULIP, MURILLO, PICOTEE, ISABELLA, BOUTON D'OR, YELLOW ROSE, POTTEBAKKER WHITE, POTTEBAKKER SCARLET, and GESNERIANA, and an infinite variety. Plant in the fall. They should be planted in the same way as hyacinths, except that, as the bulbs are smaller, it is not necessary to plant them so deep. The bulbs should be underground, four inches to the bottom of the bulb, and from five to six inches apart. A little sand around each bulb is often advisable. Blooms from the middle of April to the end of May, according to the variety.

Tulip, Picotee

294

One of the most satisfactory and beautiful of the spring-flowering bulbs. It increases considerably and is very healthy, whereas the hyacinth in time dies out. Tulips come in many colors and there are both single and double, early and late-flowering varieties, also the wonderful parrot tulips which have feathered edges and combine green with other colors.

INDEX

Ageratum, combined for color effect with crimson snapdragons, 24; combined with sweet alyssum, 33-34; with Snowstorm petunia, 34; raising of from seed, 90-91.

Almond, pink double-flowering, combination of tulips and, for color arrangement, 11.

Amaranthus Abyssinicus, or lady's riding whip, 87.

Anchusa Italica, raising of, from seed, 81-82.

Annuals, description of various kinds of, and methods of raising from seed, 86-92.

Apple trees, wild, used in a wild garden, 183-184, 186.

Arborvitæ, American, sheared plants of, for evergreen exterior decoration, 62; desirability of clipping, 63; as a decoration for terraces, 159-160.

Ash trees, raising of, 108-109.

Asparagus, successful fertilization of, 134-135.

Aster beetle, remedy for, 142.

Asters, transplanting of, 22-23; fertilization of, 128.

Azalea mollis, combination of, with tulips and daphne, 11.

Barron, Leonard, expert on lawns, 49.

Bay trees, soot as a fertilizer for, 121; used for terraces, 157-158; attention required by, after being in winter quarters, 158.

Beach grass for sea-side lawns, 49

Beech trees, time for setting out, 10.

Birds, wild gardens a home for, 184.

Black walnut trees, raising of, 106-108.

Blue border, the, 18-19.

Bocconia cordata, in white border. 16.

Bogs as natural nurseries for plants and shrubs, 174.

Bon Arbor, as a fertilizer, 121, 126-127; to be supplemented with water in case of dahlias, 127; used for verbenas, heliotrope, stocks, and asters, 128.

Bone meal, for grass, 45-46; value as a fertilizer for plants, 121.

Borders of herbaceous plants, 13 ff.; the white border, 16-17; the pink, 17-18; the blue, 18-19; the red, 19-20; the yellow and orange, 23-24; of white cosmos, pink and white

INDEX

INDEX

299

INDEX

INDEX

301

INDEX

Pyrethrum, varieties of, 79; raising of, from seed, 80.

Red border, the, 19–20.
Red top for lawns, 48.
Retinosporas, clipping of, 63.
Rhode Island bent for lawns, 48–49.
Rolling, advisability of frequent, for grass, 44.
Rose bugs, preventive mixture for, 140.
Rose caterpillar, the, 141.
Roses, bone meal a tonic for, 129; transplanting of wild, 178.
Rosy Morn variety of petunia, 25.
Rotting of seeds from rain, 72.
Rudbeckia, the casting out of, 30.

Salpiglossis, 27, 88–89; sheep manure for fertilizing, 129.
Salvia azurea grandiflora, 83–84.
Schizanthus, 27; description of, 89; suitable for adornment of terraces, 155–156.
Scotch soot as a fertilizer for foliage plants, 133.
Sea-side lawns, 49.
Seed, raising flowers from, 71 ff.; raising trees from, 97 ff.
Seed-pods, preventing formation of, 15–16.
Seeds, causes of failures of, 72–73; directions for sowing, of deciduous trees, 112–113.
Shadow pond, the, in a wild garden, 184–185.

Sheep manure, as a fertilizer for perennials, 122; for Japanese anemones, 129.
Shrubbery, combinations which can be used in, 11 ff.
Shrubs, bogs and swamps as nurseries for, 174; transplanting of, in winter, 175.
Silver King variety of German iris, 145.
Snapdragons, combination of crimson and ageratum, for color effect, 24; raising from seed, 90; successful fertilization of, 123–124.
Snowstorm variety of petunia, 24–25; combination of ageratum and, for color effect, 34.
Sod, the need for and procuring of, 55–57.
Solomon's seal, 169.
Soot, as a fertilizer, 121; for foliage plants, 133; the best fertilizer for bay and box trees, 158.
Spireas in white border, 16.
Spring garden, planting the, 9–13, 31–33.
Starwort, varieties, colors, and raising of, 80–81.
Stocks, starting of, in hotbeds, 90; fertilizing, 128.
Summer cypress, 88.
Sunlight Sash, the, 93.
Swamp maple, the, 168.
Swamps, as nurseries for plants and shrubs, 174.
Sweet peas, sowing of, 21.
Sycamore, raising from seed, 109

INDEX

303

INDEX

THE following pages contain advertisements of books by the same author or on kindred subjects.

By HELENA RUTHERFURD ELY

A Woman's Hardy Garden

With illustrations from photographs by Prof. C. F. Chandler

Cloth, illustrated, 12mo, $1.75 net, by mail $1.87

"Mrs. Ely gives copious details of the cost of plants, the exact dates of planting, the number of plants required in a given space for beauty of effect and advantage to free growth, the protection needed from sun and frost, the precautions to take against injury from insects, the satisfaction to be expected from the different varieties of plants in the matter of luxuriant bloom and length of time for blossoming, and much information to be appreciated only by those who have raised a healthy garden by the slow teaching of personal experience."—*New York Times' Saturday Review.*

"Mrs. Ely is the wisest and most winning teacher of the fascinating art of gardening that we have met in modern print."
—*New York Tribune.*

Another Hardy Garden Book

Illustrated with 49 full-page plates.

Cloth, 12mo, $1.75 net, by mail, $1.88

"Mrs. Ely's new "Hardy Garden Book" is a practical book for the amateur, telling simply about the raising of vegetables and the cultivation of fruits for the home garden. There is a chapter on trees, naming the hardiest and most rapid-growing varieties, and also giving directions for transplanting the trees, shrubs and vines to be found in woodlands and pastures. A chapter is devoted to perennials and annuals, which tells incidentally of a garden where each border is planted with flowers of one color only.

"The great value of 'Another Hardy Garden Book' lies in the fact that it deals with the conditions of soil and climate to be found in this part of the country, it narrates actual experiences in a garden not so far beyond the average city dweller as to discourage him, and it gives just the advice and information needed by the amateur gardener of moderate means and limited responsibilities."—*Philadelphia Ledger.*

PUBLISHED BY

THE MACMILLAN COMPANY

64-66 Fifth Avenue, New York

BOOKS OF GENERAL INTEREST

A Self-Supporting Home

By KATE V. ST. MAUR   *Cloth, Illustrated, 12mo, $1.75 net*

Each chapter is the detailed account of all the work necessary for one month—in the vegetable garden, among the small fruits, with the fowls, guineas, rabbits, cavies, and in every branch of husbandry to be met with on the small farm. The book is especially valuable and simple for the beginner, who has no chance to worry or grow confused about what he should do in each season.

"One of the most sensible, practical books of the kind ever published."—*Louisville Courier-Journal.*

The Earth's Bounty

By KATE V. ST. MAUR   *Cloth, Illustrated, 12mo, $1.75 net*

The present volume, though in no sense dependent on "A Self-Supporting Home," is in a sense a sequel to it. The feminine owner is still the heroine, and the new book chronicles the events after success permitted her to acquire more land and put to practical test the ideas gleaned from observation and reading.

The Fat of the Land: The Story of an American Farm

By JOHN WILLIAMS STREETER   *Cloth, 12mo, $1.50 net*

The Fat of the Land is the sort of book that ought to be epoch-making in its character, for it tells what can be accomplished through the application of business methods to the farming business. Never was the freshness, the beauty, the joy, the freedom of country life put in a more engaging fashion. From cover to cover it is a fascinating book, practical withal, and full of common sense.

Three Acres and Liberty

By BOLTON HALL   *Cloth, Illustrated, 12mo, $1.75 net*

Possibilities of the small suburban farm, and practical suggestions to city dwellers how to acquire and make profitable use of them.

PUBLISHED BY

THE MACMILLAN COMPANY
64-66 FIFTH AVENUE, NEW YORK

How to Keep Bees for Profit

By D. E. LYON *Cloth, Illustrated, 12mo, $1.50 net*

Dr. Lyon is an enthusiast on bees. He has devoted many years to the acquisition of knowledge on this subject, which, as every one who has ever followed it knows, grows more and more fascinating as one goes deeper and deeper into its mysteries. His forthcoming work is a practical one. In it he takes up the numerous questions that confront the man who keeps bees, and deals with them from the standpoint of long experience.

How to Keep Hens for Profit

By C. S. VALENTINE *Cloth, Illustrated, 12mo, $1.50 net*

There is an enormous amount of sound information which is certain to be of the greatest assistance to all who have the opportunity to raise poultry. Mr. Valentine is a well-known authority upon the subject. He is not a victim of extravagant optimism, nor has he been driven by the wild statements of others to the opposite extreme. His knowledge of the whole field is both extensive and accurate; the information that he gives will be of service, not only to the amateur who keeps poultry for his own pleasure, but to the man who wishes to derive from it a considerable portion of his income.

Manual of Gardening

By L. H. BAILEY *Cloth, Illustrated, 12mo, $2.00 net*

This new work is a combination and revision of the main parts of two other books by the same author, *Garden Making* and *Practical Garden-Book*, together with much new material and the results of the experience of ten added years. Among the persons who collaborated in the preparation of the other two books, and whose contributions have been freely used in this one, are C. E. Hunn, a gardener of long experience; Professor Ernest Walker, reared as a commercial florist; Professor L. R. Taft, and Professor F. A. Waugh, well known for their studies and writings on horticultural subjects.

The Book of Vegetables and Garden Herbs

By ALLEN FRENCH *Cloth, Illustrated, 12mo, $1.75 net*

A practical book "from the ground up." It gives complete directions for growing all vegetables cultivable in the climate of the northern United States. It represents a departure in vegetable-garden literature. It does not generalize. Leaving the description of garden processes to the general handbooks, it considers the vegetables not in classes but individually, according to their importance. The illustrations, numbering about 150, are all from original drawings, and are designed to exhibit at their best the various plants, roots, fruits, and planting methods described. They are exceedingly helpful as well as entertaining.

PUBLISHED BY

THE MACMILLAN COMPANY
64-66 FIFTH AVENUE, NEW YORK

BOOKS ON AGRICULTURE

On Selection of Land, etc.

Thomas F. Hunt's How to Choose a Farm . .	$1 75 net
E. W. Hilgard's Soils: Their Formation and Relations to Climate and Plant Growth	4 00 net
Isaac P. Roberts' The Farmstead	1 50 net

On Tillage, etc.

F. H. King's The Soil	1 50 net
Isaac P. Roberts' The Fertility of the Land .	1 50 net
Elwood Mead's Irrigation Institutions .	1 25 net
F. H. King's Irrigation and Drainage . . .	1 50 net
William E. Smythe's The Conquest of Arid America	1 50 net
Edward B. Voorhees' Fertilizers	1 25 net
Edward B. Voorhees' Forage Crops . . .	1 50 net
H. Snyder's Chemistry of Plant and Animal Life .	1 25 net
H. Snyder's Soil and Fertilizers. Third edition	1 25 net
L. H. Bailey's Principles of Agriculture . . .	1 25 net
W. C. Welborn's Elements of Agriculture, Southern and Western	75 net
J. F. Duggar's Agriculture for Southern Schools	75 net
G. F. Warren's Elements of Agriculture . . .	1 10 net
T. L. Lyon and E. O. Fippen's The Principles of Soil Management	1 75 net
Hilgard & Osterhout's Agriculture for Schools on the Pacific Slope	1 00 net
J. A. Widtsoe's Dry Farming . .	1 50 net

On Garden-Making

L. H. Bailey's Manual of Gardening . .	2 00 net
L. H. Bailey's Vegetable-Gardening . .	1 50 net
L. H. Bailey's Horticulturist's Rule Book .	75 net
L. H. Bailey's Forcing Book .	1 25 net
A. French's Book of Vegetables	1 75 net

On Fruit-Growing, etc.

L. H. Bailey's Nursery Book . . .	1 50 net
L. H. Bailey's Fruit-Growing	1 50 net
L. H. Bailey's The Pruning Book	1 50 net
F. W. Card's Bush Fruits	1 50 net
J. T. Bealby's Fruit Ranching in British Columbia.	1 50 net

On the Care of Live Stock

D. E. Lyon's How to Keep Bees for Profit .	1 50 net
Nelson S. Mayo's The Diseases of Animals .	1 50 net
W. H. Jordan's The Feeding of Animals .	1 50 net
I. P. Roberts' The Horse	1 25 net
George C. Watson's Farm Poultry	1 25 net
C. S. Valentine's How to Keep Hens for Profit . .	1 50 net
O. Kellner's The Scientific Feeding of Animals (trans.)	1 90 net
M. H. Reynolds' Veterinary Studies for Agricultural Students	1 75 net

On Dairy Work

Henry H. Wing's Milk and its Products $1 50 net
C. M. Aikman's Milk   1 25 net
Harry Snyder's Dairy Chemistry   1 00 net
W. D. Frost's Laboratory Guide in Elementary Bacteriology   1 60 net
I. P. Sheldon's The Farm and the Dairy   1 00 net
Chr. Barthel's Methods Used in the Examination of Milk and Dairy Products   1 90 net

On Plant Diseases, etc.

George Massee's Plant Diseases   1 60 net
J. G. Lipman's Bacteria in Relation to Country Life   1 50 net
E. C. Lodeman's The Spraying of Plants   1 25 net
H. M. Ward's Diseases in Plants (English)   1 60 net
A. S. Packard's A Text-book on Entomology   4 50 net

On Production of New Plants

L. H. Bailey's Plant-Breeding   1 25 net
L. H. Bailey's The Survival of the Unlike   2 00 net
L. H. Bailey's The Evolution of Our Native Fruits   2 00 net
W. S. Harwood's New Creations in Plant Life   1 75 net

On Economics and Organization

J. McLennan's Manual of Practical Farming   1 50 net
L. H. Bailey's The State and the Farmer   1 25 net
Henry C. Taylor's Agricultural Economics   1 25 net
I. P. Roberts' The Farmer's Business Handbook   1 25 net
George T. Fairchild's Rural Wealth and Welfare   1 25 net
S. E. Sparling's Business Organization. (In the Citizen's Library. Includes a chapter on Farming)   1 25 net
Kate V. St. Maur's A Self-Supporting Home   1 75 net
Kate V. St. Maur's The Earth's Bounty   1 75 net
G. F. Warren and K. C. Livermore's Exercises in Farm-Management   80 net
H. N. Ogden's Rural Hygiene   1 50 net

On Everything Agricultural

L. H. Bailey's Cyclopedia of American Agriculture:
Vol. I. Farms, Climates, and Soils.
Vol. II. Farm Crops.
Vol. III. Farm Animals.
Vol. IV. The Farm and the Community.

Complete in four royal 8vo volumes, with over 2,000 illustrations. Price of sets; cloth, $20 net; half-morocco, $32 net.

For further information as to any of the above, address the publishers.

PUBLISHED BY

THE MACMILLAN COMPANY

64-66 FIFTH AVENUE, NEW YORK

THE RURAL OUTLOOK SET

By PROF. L. H. BAILEY, Director of the New York State College of Agriculture at Cornell University

Four volumes. Each, cloth, 12mo. Uniform binding, attractively boxed. Each volume also sold separately.

In this set are included three of Professor Bailey's most popular books as well as a hitherto unpublished one,—"The Country-Life Movement." The long and persistent demand for a uniform edition of these little classics is answered with the publication of this attractive series.

The Country-Life Movement

This hitherto unpublished volume deals with the present movement for the re-direction of rural civilization, discussing the real country-life problem as distinguished from the city problem, known as the back-to-the-land movement.

The Outlook to Nature (New and revised edition)

In this alive and bracing book, full of suggestion and encouragement, Professor Bailey argues the importance of contact with nature, a sympathetic attitude toward which "means greater efficiency, hopefulness, and repose."

The State and the Farmer (New edition)

It is the relation of the farmer to the government that Professor Bailey here discusses in its varying aspects. He deals specifically with the change in agricultural methods, in the shifting of the geographical centers of farming in the United States, and in the growth of agricultural institutions.

The Nature Study Idea (New edition)

"It would be well," the critic of *The Tribune Farmer* once wrote, "If 'The Nature Study Idea' were in the hands of every person who favors nature study in the public schools, of every one who is opposed to it, and, most important, of every one who teaches it or thinks he does." It has been Professor Bailey's purpose to interpret the new school movement to put the young into relation and sympathy with nature,—a purpose which he has admirably accomplished.

PUBLISHED BY

THE MACMILLAN COMPANY

64-66 FIFTH AVENUE, NEW YORK

Lightning Source UK Ltd.
Milton Keynes UK
UKHW010155020522
402332UK00001B/154